Hands down the best bang for your marketing bucks! Angela and Dorothy keep sharing the magazine with all my prospects. I consider them my personal marketing team!

Catherine Vu
Pro-Active IT Management Inc.
www.proactiveit.ca

Womanition Paid For Itself In One Week!
Ooh la la ladies! A *big* thank you for what you've done with *Womanition*. Within *one week* I had attracted two new clients as well as a major media interview. The ad paid for itself immediately!

Kim Duke
CEO of The Sales Divas
www.salesdivas.com
Sherwood Park, AB

Womanition magazine was a great way to promote myself in the community. The visual presentation was professional and well laid out. I had very positive feedback from customers and it gave me the added exposure that worked well with my media campaign.

Kim Deep, CMA
Kidz Make Cents Inc.
www.kidzmakecents.com

Being featured in the *Womanition* magazine has been a wonderful experience. It is such a professional magazine that it has enhanced my credibility as an entrepreneur and has certainly increased my visibility as well! The team at *Womanition* offers great support and extra benefits all the while offering a fun experience to their advertisers.

Michelle La Rue
People Person
Clever by Design
www.cleverbydesign.ca
(780) 485-7863 • michelle@cleverbydesign.ca

Womanition is an outstanding resource to create awareness of both yourself and your business. Being featured in a superior publication alongside other successful business women only serves to provide further creditability and clarity in the marketplace.

Jo-Ann Vacing
eWomenNetwork
eWomenNetwork.com
jo-annvacing@shaw.ca

In 2007 I took the opportunity to appear in your first *Womanition* magazine. I am still getting business calls two years later—and still love the concept of Womanition empowering women.

Heather Bell
Baseline Management Ltd.
E-Mail:blmgt@shaw.ca

As a member of Womanition, I have found myself, on several occasions, handing over to friends and acquaintances information on businesses I have come across or read about in the *Womanition* magazines. I have had a profound response from all—thanking me for introducing them to those businesses as well as requesting as to how they may obtain copies of the magazine. It has proven beneficial to my company in getting the word out on clean and healthy water and, as a businesswoman, it is truly my pleasure to be listed among these women in business.

Karen Thomas
Home Water Systems Inc.
(offering 30 day free trials)
www.homewatersystems.ca

Womanition is an extremely effective way to reach out, show and tell, as it were. When people can see who they are dealing with and get to know through the printed page, it makes the first handshake more like a reunion hug of sorts.

Debra Cookson
Academy of Reflexology
Have Feet Will Travel,
www.reflexacademy.cs

Getting my message, Financial Independence for Women, out to the public had been a difficult one until I started publishing my articles in the *Womanition* magazine! Many women have responded to the articles, met with me, and now have a financial plan to help secure their future.

Donna Worthington CFP EPC
Investment Planning Counsel
Certified Financial Planner

These two exquisite professionals understand marketing for women to women and are the ones who do it best with Womanition. Dororthy and Angela are more than "women in process"—they are women in action!
With gratitude,

Erin Walter
Erin Walter Insurance
Wealth Expert
www.beprotected.biz

I was featured in the 2008 *Womanition* magazine and have had great response and contacts. This has help me in my business in many, many ways. Thank you, *Womanition*.

Brenda Topley
Black Sheep Design Studio
www.bstdesignstudio.com

As a result of the *Womanition* feature, people are now recognizing me and calling me by my first name. Asked how they knew my name, they reply, "I saw you in a magazine." *Womanition* has given me my Brand. Thank you.

Connie John
2 Rooms
connie.john1@gmail.com

WOMEN IN PROCESS

WOMANITION™

presents

WOMEN IN PROCESS

Forever Books

WINNIPEG MB CANADA
www.foreverbooks.ca

ISBN: 978-0-9783781-7-2
Printed in Canada
Photos by:
Daphne Carlyle, MPA SPA

Victor B. Tucker

TUCKER
PHOTOGRAPHY

Managing Editor: Beryl Henne
Typesetting: Andrew Mackay
Cover Design: Awe Creative

Published by: Forever Books
Winnipeg, MB Canada
www.foreverbooks.ca

TABLE OF CONTENTS

FROM THE FOUNDERS

The *Heart* of Womanition™
is to support women and children in need.

The *Business* of Womanition™
is to support and promote women in business.

DOROTHY BRIGGS

Womanition™ magazine provides a unique, exciting, and very effective venue for women to market and promote themselves and their business. We also provide the same opportunity for male-owned businesses to market to women, the fastest growing market in North America—both economically and numerically.

"If we build it, they will come" is not realistic. Advertising and marketing is crucial to our success. We need to target the right market and make sure our resources are spent to their fullest advantage.

Womanition™ is the answer.

We are all about women, directed to women, and supporting women. We understand the importance of stretching your marketing dollars so we go beyond the magazine to promote you and your business by offering an extra (or sometimes, only) on-line presence, building a community of like-minded business-women who support and promote each others' businesses and are introducing Womanition™ sponsored networking/educational luncheons across the city. These are all opportunities for you to "get out there" and invite the world to come knocking at your door!

If this is your first introduction to Womanition™, welcome to our team!

If you are already part of our team, thank you!

"If nothing is sold, nothing happens."

ANGELA SLADEN

It's all about people.
People before anything.
People are what make life worth living.
People are what matter.

As you meet the many wonderful women in this new anthology of Womanition™, I am sure you will relate on many levels with them. Business is all about relationships.

Our goal is that you will create many new personal and business relationships as you catch a peek into these business leaders' lives and discover why they do what they do.

MARKETING TO WOMEN

Your Most Significant &
Profitable Opportunity!

DID YOU KNOW?

85% of all monies in the economy are spent by women
They buy for their families, for their businesses, for the businesses they work for
They influence the larger family purchases
In short, they buy, buy, buy!

94% of all home furnishings are bought by women
89% of vacation decisions are made by women
80% of home improvements are initiated by women
80% of all health care is decided by women
75% of new homes are chosen by women
66% of all personal computers are bought by women
55% of all consumer electronics are bought by women
53% of used cars are purchased or leased by women

WHY MARKET TO WOMEN?

Women talk; they are great multipliers. They spread the word, good or bad. Referrals are *free* advertising! Women are loyal. Give women what they want and they are with you as a client for life; ignore their needs and pay the price in lost revenue. Women are the #1 Economic Opportunity and the Best Kept Secret!

WHAT ARE THE DIFFERENCES IN THE WAY WOMEN BUY?

Women are "equal brained"—thinking more evenly with both hemispheres. It's been said that women are great multitaskers.

Women's senses and emotions are more sensitive and intense. Be kind and considerate, not mushy. Keep your place of business smelling clean, not smelling like perfume. Women notice the details.

Women are synthesists; they put things together, piece by piece. Does the information you are giving your women clients jive? Being very intuitive, women can smell a rat or a misrepresentation. Women are people powered. Develop a relationship before an invoice.

Women are verbally inclined. Women like to be talked to, not down to. Talk to them about things they care about. Sell the benefit your product or service will do for them and the things they care about.

WHAT DO WOMEN THINK AND CARE ABOUT?

Women care about relationships with their husbands, children, grandchildren, friends, parents—basically everyone they interact with, including you and your business.

Women like warm, caring, and considerate people. Women care about their children's accomplishments and well-being. Women care about a warm, comfortable, and orderly home. The number one investment full-time working women make is in a great housekeeper.

Women care about their appearance; looking the best they can. Women take pride in their ability to empathize and act on it. If they see a need, they want to help and therefore make the world a better place. Women like being needed.

Women enjoy challenges and achievements. They like to learn and progress. Home Depot has done a wonderful job fulfilling this desire in women through their free "courses and classes." Women enjoy working, whether at home or in the work place. Being recognized for our productivity is very important.

WHAT WOMEN DON'T ENJOY!

Women do not enjoy feeling isolated or lonely. Women don't care how much you know, they need to know how much you care. Women are not too concerned with facts and features; they care about benefits that your products and services will bring to them and the people they care about. They care that your products work, not how they work.

WHAT DO WOMEN EXPECT?

Women are open to help, advice, and others' opinions. That doesn't mean they are pushovers, just willing to hear you out. It is all about relationships. Women are open to emotion. They care about how your product or service makes them feel or how it makes the people they care about feel. Will it add value to them and their relationships?

Women expect care and consideration in their dealings. If they feel slighted, they're outta here!

WHAT WILL IT TAKE FOR YOUR BUSINESS TO CAPTURE THIS EXPLODING MARKET?

Be sure not to miss one single Marketing to Women luncheon workshops sponsored by Womanition™. If you would like to attend these informative networking luncheons, please e-mail angela@womanition.com with "luncheons" in the subject line.

If you would like a more personalized business application, please e-mail with "personalized application" in the subject line.

WOMANITION™

presents

WOMEN IN PROCESS

OVERCOMING BARRIERS

Jennifer Belland
Mortgage Professional

It takes "a certain kind of person" to succeed in self-employment, Jennifer Belland says, "a person who can overcome barriers." She should know. She has overcome many.

"I didn't think higher education was an option for me growing up," Jennifer says. "I grew up very poor in a trailer park in Edmonton, with parents who struggled to make ends meet. My background is largely from the school of hard knocks."

Early on, she realized it would be up to her to take care of herself. She sometimes had trouble staying awake in class because she had gone to school hungry, but even then she had "an internal motivation, a thought that there was something more out there. I knew I was capable of doing something more." She saw other people living happy, fulfilled lives, and she wanted that for herself.

Jennifer moved out on her own at age sixteen. Shortly after this, her mother received a promotion at her job and moved out of province. Somehow, Jennifer held down two part-time jobs and still managed to maintain excellent grades in high school. After graduation, she left Alberta for ten months and completed her first year at Memorial University of Newfoundland. At Memorial, she enrolled in Germanic Studies with a minor in Biology, and chose Newfoundland out of shear adventure. Upon returning to Alberta, she had to take a year off due to a serious accident involving her bicycle and a motor vehicle. After her recovery, she managed to hold a nearly full-time job while taking a full course load at the University of Alberta, but switched specialties, eventually awarded a BA in Women's Studies. She learned a lot, but looking back, suggests, "I didn't know whether I wanted to go into the Arts or the Sciences. Clearly a great fit for me would have been Commerce. I feel I've always had a knack for it."

After graduation, Jennifer continued working at the same job for the next nine years. She says, "I really didn't know what I wanted to do. I just knew I wanted to do something more."

Then in 2002, she was diagnosed with multiple sclerosis (MS). "That explained why my body was not cooperating with me all the time," Jennifer says. "I decided to use that as a reason to leave the safety and security of my job. I thought that would really light a fire under me to make me find out what I wanted to do."

She then bought a house, intending to spend a year renovating and flipping it, hoping that she would make some money in this way, and that by the time this project was finished she would know what she wanted to do. But she grew attached to the house and has kept it as a revenue property.

A month after completing the renovations, in October 2002, she took a class in scrapbooking. At the end of the class, the instructor said there was an opportunity for others to get involved in the business. Jennifer saw the opportunity and grabbed it. For the next five years she ran her own business as a Creative Memories consultant. She says, "I loved the scrapbooking business. I was very passionate about helping people preserve their photographs and family stories. Perhaps in part because my family had not stayed together permanently, it was important for me to see families use their photo albums to celebrate being together."

Being self-employed also made it easier to handle her health problems since there was less stress when she had to take time off for health reasons.

A turning point came a couple years later, after overlapping, back-to-back relapses with her MS. "I decided I was sick and tired of being sick and tired," Jennifer recalls. "I declared myself healthy. I said I accept that my body has MS, but as my identity, I don't." Jennifer was not going to ignore the disease, but she decided she was not going to let it control her life either. She stepped down from her extensive volunteer work with the MS Society and concentrated on other things. She has been healthy ever since.

Jennifer married in 2003, but the marriage didn't last. She and her husband separated a month before their daughter was born, and were divorced in 2007. It was a difficult time, but they are still "good friends." Looking to start over, Jennifer moved to Calgary.

This could have been the low point of Jennifer's life. Instead, it became what she sees as her greatest personal victory. "I relocated to a new city, started a new relationship, and took on a new career—all with a newborn baby."

She started a new career as a mortgage professional. She was ready for a change, and her new partner, a mortgage broker, convinced her that she would be good at it because she was "great with people and super organized." Jennifer says, "I can work with all kinds of people from different kinds of backgrounds."

It turned out her partner was right. Jennifer became a self-employed mortgage professional affiliated with Mortgage Alliance (www.albertamortgagequotes.com/jenniferbelland) and has done very well in her new career—so well that she discontinued her scrapbooking business in January 2008. In a slumping housing market, when some other agents are having to find different jobs, Jennifer is getting busier. She has gone out and found clients, including some from her previous scrapbooking business.

Most of her clients have come from her own initiative including joining various groups and networking. As well, she is already getting repeat business and referrals. "I must be doing something right," she says.

Being a mortgage professional is like being a realtor, Jennifer says. "I have to sell myself and my name."

Part of her success comes from being prepared. Besides the Mortgage Alliance's own RightMortgage™ product, Jennifer offers many different mortgage products from over forty different financial institutions. In a challenging market, the financial institutions are changing their products all the time, trying to remain competitive, introducing new programs and tightening the restrictions on other programs. Jennifer keeps up with all these changes, the Bank of Canada rate, and what's going on in the housing market.

In all of her careers, Jennifer says, "I took as much training as I could. When I take something on, I like to be an expert in it if I can, to go above and beyond." Regarding the constant changes in her new field, she says, "I don't *have* to keep up. I *choose* to keep up. I want to know that I'm giving great guidance to my clients."

While only a small percentage of people use a mortgage professional, that percentage is growing, and much of that growth is due to "word of mouth"—satisfied clients (sometimes saving thousands of dollars) are telling other people about their experience. Mortgage professionals often save their clients time and effort; they fill out one application form with Jennifer instead of filling out a different form at each financial institution.

Jennifer is determined to give "great service" to her clients. "People don't get automated voice mail when they call me. They don't leave a message and wait three days before they get a call back."

But there is more to it than that. "There has to be an element of trust built up," Jennifer says. That is where her people skills come in and her ability to really understand and connect with people. While men tend to be more focused on business, "women tend to be more into relationship building," she says. If someone is asking for a mortgage worth hundreds of thousands of dollars, it is crucial to trust the mortgage professional you're dealing with.

"Some people are more entrepreneurial than others. Some people need a regular paycheck," Jennifer says. "Being self-employed takes a certain kind of person—self-motivated, accountable, responsible, knowing how to punch your own clock." This means working hard but also knowing not to work too many hours. You have to make your work time as productive and efficient as possible.

Jennifer loves what she is doing now. She feels great when she can help clients save thousands of dollars or obtain a first mortgage after they have been turned down by a bank. "Sometimes there is no reason why they can't get a mortgage. It's just that a particular lender didn't have a program that they fit into. A lot of my clients are self-employed people who hear through word of mouth that a mortgage professional will often get them a better rate than the banks will give them." Having grown up poor, then renting for many years, she finds it especially rewarding to "help people get into their own home" and "help young people transition to home ownership." Sometimes this involves showing young people that their mortgage payment will be not much more than they are currently paying in rent, "showing people what's possible." Jennifer adds, "I'm pretty big on possibility."

Jennifer is passionate about both scrapbooking and mortgage brokering because both careers have very positive aspects. In both positions, she has been able to focus on "what I am capable of" and "what I can do for others."

Her goal has been to "get to a point where I can give back instead of focusing on just surviving." When you're in survival mode, "all your energy goes to wondering when you're going to get your next paycheck or how you're going to put food on the table," Jennifer says. "For me, success is not making more money or having more things, but getting to a point where you're not only working on your career and building your family, but you have time to contribute back to others."

Now expecting her second child, Jennifer enjoys being able to work from home and intersperse work with family responsibilities. She also much prefers being free to make her own decisions. "I can do it when I want, how I want." And the financial rewards are greater. "Having my own business, the only cap to my income is myself. I'm in control of it. What I put in I get out." This wasn't true of her time as an employee, for instance, where promotions and pay raises were normally based on numbers of hours worked. "You could be the best salesperson or the fastest and friendliest cashier and bring in repeat business, but there was no reward for greater effort."

While eager to help others, Jennifer can look back on times when others have helped her. For example, she was able to watch her mother in action at work. "She was a pretty good businesswoman. She was definitely highly motivated and focused." At a time when most managers were men, "I saw her as a woman able to overcome the barriers for women in management."

Jennifer remembers a special elementary school teacher, Mr. Potter. When things were difficult at Jennifer's home, he took time to talk to her at recess and tell her that she was smart and beautiful, and that he believed in her. It made a great difference in her life. Later on, as an adult, she went back to thank him, but couldn't find him. She would be happy if she could give the same kind of support and inspiration to others.

Jennifer found many women who inspired her in the Women's Studies program. She learned about a lot of great women who overcame barriers to get the vote, to achieve equality and various rights. She notes, "That wasn't so long ago."

Donna Worthington, a financial planner Jennifer met at the Women's Show in Edmonton, has helped her greatly. She still works with Donna today.

Jennifer also continues to educate herself and pursue personal development. She reads books such as Eckhart Tolle's *The Power of Now* and books by Malcolm Gladwell and Debbie Ford. "I love to learn."

Jennifer says, "I found my passion when I became aware I was responsible and accountable for my own life." She mentions Landmark Education courses (www.landmarkeducation.com) that showed her she had to design her own life. She adds, "The more open-minded I am, the more I explore things, the more courses I take for personal development and personal growth, the more I learn about myself and human beings, the more alive I feel, the more connected I feel with the world, and the more I want to share with others what I have learned."

Jennifer is passionate about a lot of things—playing classical piano, going to concerts, enjoying nature, nurturing her growing family, inspiring and empowering others.

Asked what her biggest mistake was, Jennifer suggests, "not having faith in myself sooner, to take chances and do what I'm doing now sooner in life." But she adds that mistakes often lead to learning big lessons. "I don't really have regrets. I did the best I could at the time. I wouldn't do anything over."

Asked what advice she would give others, Jennifer offers two quotations that have inspired her: "It's time to start living the life you've imagined" (Henry James), and "Just keep swimming" (from the movie *Finding Nemo*).

But she offers some of her own thoughts as well. "Success is not something you find. It's something you be"—being leads to doing, and doing leads to having. Jennifer says it is the wrong approach to think you will be happy if you keep working at a job you don't really like in order to buy material things or become someone different. Instead, "choose to be happy, then do things in alignment with that, and it will lead to success. See yourself as successful. Ask yourself what successful people do, and then do that." She explains that once you realize you are successful, it will change things—you might find you don't need those material items or image to be happy after all.

Never Give Up

Dorothy Briggs
Co-founder, Owner, Publisher of Womanition

Dorothy Briggs knows exactly how and when she became an entrepreneur. She was fourteen, the second oldest of eight children, and her mother told her she couldn't afford to buy her new shoes. That just made Dorothy more determined to have them. "I don't take no for an answer," she says. She got three jobs—scooping ice cream, shampooing hair, and waiting tables—and within about two weeks she had the shoes.

That incident taught Dorothy a lesson that has guided her life. "I realized that if I wanted something that had a price tag, I had to go get it because no one was going to get it for me ... I never had anything given to me. I've had to work for everything I've got."

Dorothy has no formal higher education—just "street training." She has never had a formal mentor, but has learned by watching others. She says, "My philosophy is show me, don't tell me. That's how I've learned to do things."

After high school, with no obvious career ahead of her, Dorothy started to look around for "work I could do." Sales seemed an obvious choice. She soon got a job at Woolco. Within a month, she was managing a department. "I was getting angry because I had to make decisions, but I couldn't make decisions because there was no manager," she says. "So they made me the manager."

This was followed by a series of jobs and business projects, from owning and operating clothing stores in Brandon and The Pas, Manitoba, to selling real estate. She also published *Builder Architect* magazine in Kelowna, British Columbia and Calgary, Alberta, for three-and-a-half years and a health and wellness magazine for four-and-a-half years. She says, "Every business I've had, I started with no money, no operating capital—but I paid all my bills. I have a huge belief in myself. I was always very determined and competitive. My friends all say I am a very gentle person, but I can be assertive too."

None of this was easy. "Retail is hard," she laughs. "I pick everything hard. My jobs, my careers have all been hard."

Perhaps that is deliberate. "I have to have a challenge," Dorothy says. "I have to keep my mind constantly going. I have to be doing something."

One of the most difficult assignments Dorothy ever undertook turned out to be one of her greatest accomplishments. On this project, she had three weeks to sell 10,000 dollars in ads for the *Builder/Architect* publication. Once she started, she discovered that the leads she had been given weren't panning out; people were slamming down the phone. "I cried every day for three weeks." But her niece, Lisa Huston, gave her Napoleon Hill's book *Think and Grow Rich*, and it inspired her not to give up. At the end of the three weeks, she had sold 10,400 dollars in ads. "It was the hardest thing I ever did, but it showed me that I could do anything." The owner of *Builder/Architect* magazine later asked her why she hadn't just quit when things got so hard. She answered that she had given her word that she would stay and get the job done, so she did.

Dorothy takes the same approach in all parts of her life. When she moved to Calgary and wanted to buy a house, she had only 1,000 dollars but needed 20,000 dollars for a down payment. She handed over what she had and said she would have the rest within six months. Six months later, she had the rest of the money and closed the deal. "I knew I could do it because all I had to do is go out and sell more." It was hard, she did without drapes and a lot of other things for a year, but she got what she wanted.

Dorothy recalls, from her real estate career, "December is supposed to be the worst month in real estate, but Decembers were my biggest month." Nobody told her it was a bad month for sales, so she just kept selling.

SELLING AND MORE

Common to all of Dorothy's positions and businesses is a marketing element. "I just know how to sell. I know how to make people believe what I am saying. If I believe in something, I can sell you on it." Yet she describes herself as "an entrepreneur" rather than a salesperson or marketer. "I won't do it unless I think it is good for you. I would never talk someone into something that wasn't right for them. Never sell somebody something they don't want. You have to interview them and find out what they need. You do it for them, not yourself."

The key is to have integrity in dealing with customers, Dorothy says. "I mean what I say, and I take care of my clients." The best route is to under-promise and over-deliver: "They get the 'wow' factor from me. If I don't 'wow' my customers, I'm not doing my job. Sometimes I've made promises to people and afterward I wondered why I had done that. But I stuck to my word, and I did it."

Something else Dorothy is good at is solving problems. "If there is an issue, I deal with it immediately. That could be why I have been very successful at most of the things I do, because I don't have issues. I deal with them, and then they're gone and they never come up again. If there is a misunderstanding or if someone doesn't want to pay a bill, I will make arrangements and negotiate with them until I get paid for the work I have done."

Another key to Dorothy's success is her willingness to take the initiative. "When I walk down the street, I smile at people. I don't wait for somebody to do something for me. I do something first." She quotes the proverb, "Losers let things happen to them. Winners make things happen."

"I don't waste time," Dorothy continues. When she is with a client, "I don't talk an hour when I can do it in half an hour. I get to the point." She says men especially appreciate the direct approach. "If you're direct and professional, people want to do business with you." The direct approach shows confidence, that "you know what you've got and what it will do for them."

WOMANITION

All of these experiences prepared Dorothy for her current main enterprise, Womanition, which she founded, along with business partner, editor, and co-owner Angela Sladen. Womanition offers how-to articles (written by experts in various fields), teaching seminars, and other resources to women.

Networking is an important aspect of Womanition, Dorothy says. "The women support each other, and we give each other leads and give each other business."

Central to this enterprise is the annual *Womanition* magazine, which profiles and promotes women entrepreneurs and women in business. Womanition gives the women an opportunity to promote their businesses and market their products through the magazine, through the Womanition website (www.womanition.com) and through Womanition trade shows.

The intent of the profiles, Dorothy says, is to present women as human beings who have families, who have overcome obstacles, and who have accomplished wonderful things. "When women are profiled in a magazine, it gives them huge credibility. People will perceive that this person must be successful, she must know what she's doing, and I'm going to call her if I need whatever service or product she is offering."

Womanition also offers an opportunity for others to market to women—through advertising in *Womanition* magazine, for instance. This is one of the most significant and profitable opportunities for businesses, Dorothy says, because 85 percent of spending is done by women. However, the primary goal of the project is not to sell things to women but "to help women from start to end."

Dorothy takes pride in what she has accomplished, saying the most recent edition of *Womanition* "is my best work, as far as magazines go." It is a joy to hold the magazine in her hands, "to feel it and touch it," but it is even more gratifying "to see how it changes people's lives."

Started in Edmonton, Womanition has already expanded to Calgary/Southern Alberta and Fort McMurray. The Southern readership is over 160,000 in both Calgary and Edmonton, and Dorothy is actively seeking to franchise Womanition in major centers all across Canada.

Of course, Dorothy being Dorothy, she isn't content to have just one project on the go. She is also General Manager and business partner with two amazing programmers, James Marusiak, the Project Development Manager, and Alberio Bathory-Frota, the Advanced Technology Engineer, in Servall Data Systems—a software package that offers customer tracking and security services for bars and nightclubs. Servall Data Systems Inc. has developed the latest technology software suite called Intellibar that has the capability to capture Identification and Incident Tracking. Other modules included in the suite are Intellibar VIP, Intellibar Admissions, Intellibar Notifications, Intellibar Coat Check, and Intellibar Business Intelligence, and soon to come, the Intellibar Point of Sale Module will be second to none.

PASSION AND PLEASURE

Dorothy says it isn't hard to find your passion. "When you wake up in the morning and you have a choice of what to do, choose what makes you happy." She adds, "We're all motivated by something. Mine is the fear of being poor." Growing up, she remembers when a single can of salmon was all there was to feed eight people, and she doesn't want to return to that state. "I don't have a husband, and I don't have people buying me things or doing things for me." Since she doesn't rely on anyone else to pay her way, she knows it is up to her to do it.

Dorothy says, "I don't have a great interest in what I have in my bank account … I'm more interested in what I can do day-to-day." Nevertheless, she owns a new home and is becoming more financially secure.

Something else Dorothy is passionate about is protecting children. "If we wiped out child abuse, we wouldn't have all these issues, we wouldn't have all these criminals and mental problems."

For that reason, Dorothy is also passionate about giving to charities. "I've been very fortunate. I'm healthy. I have very good social skills," she says. Therefore, she is eager to give something back. She has been a Rotary member and a member of the Board of Directors of the Sherwood Park Chamber of Commerce. She was also in charge of acquisitions for the Calgary Homebuilders Foundation for three years, receiving enough donations of goods to raise 160,000 dollars in a single night; the money was used to build housing for the homeless.

That passion continues today. The primary goal of Womanition, Dorothy says, is not to make money for her but to help women. To that end, Womanition has already made its first contribution to the Edmonton Dream Centre, a residential program to help addicted and abused women (www.edmonton-dreamcentre.ca). Womanition has also donated thousands of dollars to the e-women Networking Foundation, and is a huge supporter of *Womanition* magazine.

"What goes around comes around," Dorothy says. For that reason, she is determined to treat others well. She can get along even with people she doesn't like, and when others treat her badly, she has learned not to retaliate "no matter what they do."

THE BOTTOM LINE

While she has had a lot of successes to celebrate, Dorothy is also open about sharing her weaknesses.

Asked what her biggest mistake was, Dorothy replies promptly, "I did not ask enough people for help. As a matter of fact, I didn't ask anybody for help. I did a lot of things on my own, and I should have asked for help. Before, I thought I knew it all and wanted to do it my way. Big mistake. Now I ask the right questions. There are more people helping me now because I'm allowing them to." In business, "you need to know what you are doing, but in a lot of situations I didn't know what I was doing." When she was starting out, there were people she could have gone to for advice, but instead "I learned a lot on my own and wasted time and energy." She adds that if she had sought help earlier, "I probably would have wound up in the same place, but it would have been a lot less stressful. I've worked hard all my life. Now I'm working smarter."

The best single piece of advice Dorothy can offer is "Never give up." There is no question that difficulties will come, but "misfortune brings opportunities to people who hang in, wait it out, and don't give up."

BRINGING JOY THROUGH CREATIVITY

Daphne Carlyle MPA SPA
Owner, Carlyle Portraits Inc.

Daphne Carlyle has had so many successes that she enthuses, "My life journey to this point has been my success—but it's not over! I'm continuing to grow all the time. Life is not a destination; it's a journey."

But that journey started slowly, and it took Daphne quite some time to find herself. She is an only child and thinks that may "have a lot to do with who I am today." When she was nine, her parents moved to Edmonton from the small mining town of Flin Flon, Manitoba. Daphne's early years were "pretty uneventful"—school, sports, and being on student council. She earned a degree in physical education from the University of Alberta and began teaching school.

Daphne took time out to get married and have three children, then returned to teaching. At this point, she chose to teach elementary school because she "never wanted to be a high school coach." She "just loved teaching," but a crisis was looming. She finally reached a point where she was "burned out." Her marriage had become abusive and was breaking down, she was trying to balance full-time teaching with raising her own three children, and "nobody was getting the best of me—the kids at school weren't getting the best teacher, my kids didn't have the best mother, and I wasn't the best person for me."

The crisis led to "a total change," and the change was good.

Daphne left her marriage, took a leave of absence from teaching, moved away from Fort McMurray, where she had been living, and enrolled in a two-year photographic technology course at NAIT (Northern Alberta Institute of Technology) in Edmonton.

The choice of a new career was no accident. "All my life I had always had a camera," Daphne says, and, in the difficult days, photography had become her refuge. "I lived on the green belt. I could walk across for an hour and immerse myself in nature with my camera and then come back and feel refreshed." The local photo lab was very complimentary about her work, and so were her friends. "This was something I loved to do, and I thought maybe I could move on in my life with this," Daphne says. "I knew I was better than the regular snapshot taker."

The change in career was not the big thing. The internal changes were bigger than the external ones. Before the crisis, Daphne recalls, "I had a good job, I had the respect of the community, but I did not respect myself."

Daphne explains: "Our journey through life is filled with all kinds of situations which we are meant to go through and learn from. They can make you or break you." It took "lots of counseling," but Daphne finally came to a new level of understanding of her situation. "I grew from it and became stronger. I learned I was capable on my own. I discovered who I was and what my strengths were."

Ironically, after eight years alone, that new understanding of her own self-worth eventually led to "a more suitable relationship, a great partnership with a very special man"—her marriage to her current husband, Art.

But before that happened, she had to develop her own photographic career. Through NAIT and the Professional

Photographers of Canada association, Daphne had taken an extra course and gained retouching skills. In the photographic world, where most photographers operate one-person shops, many don't have retouching expertise. This enabled Daphne to get a job. Over five years, she worked for a succession of shops and "learned so much more" working with these other professionals.

Daphne especially learned a great deal from Malcolm Fraser of Fraser's Photography. He was "a wonderful teacher, one of my mentors, a great person, and a great photographer." One winter, Malcolm went skiing and broke his leg. It turned out to be Daphne's "big break" as well as Malcolm's. While he was recovering, Daphne had to "get behind the camera." Daphne felt a lot of pressure to live up to the studio's high-end reputation but says, "I knew I was capable, and I gained a lot of confidence from that."

When Malcolm came back, it was time for Daphne to establish her own small studio, Creative Visualizations, which opened in Edmonton in 1992. "I wanted it to be all mine. When you work for other people, it's just a job. I felt great ownership of the work I did, but it wasn't mine. It belonged to a studio," Daphne says. "Every artist wants to achieve recognition on her own. And I was ready to be my own person and do my own thing."

By this time, Daphne had met Art Carlyle through Professional Photographers of Canada, where they were both active members, and he encouraged her to go out on her own. Daphne is very passionate about the association and has been on the national executive. She sees it as a place where photographers can "rub shoulders with really top-notch photographers, become friends, and learn from each other."

Art was doing commercial photography and had a business doing laminating and mounting large signs and maps for commercial properties. They moved to an acreage in Strathcona County twenty minutes from Edmonton and married in 1993. Art eventually transformed his business into a Maptown franchise in Edmonton and later added a related business called Framing Matters, while Daphne continued to operate her studio, renamed Carlyle Portraits.

Daphne kept her studio in Edmonton for a year or so, thinking (wrongly it turned out) that she needed to maintain a visible presence in the city. Still, starting out on her own was hard. "Marketing is the hardest part of my job. Looking back, I don't know how I got any clients," Daphne says. "I needed a way to tell people I was here. At first, nobody knows who you are, and you're not even in the Yellow Pages for a year. You can't just sit and wait for the phone to ring." She called her friends to bring in their children for photo sessions so she could develop some samples of her work. The next thing was to "find places where people could see them. You have to be in people's face and have something to show them." She set up mall displays and talked to people, and word of mouth gradually began to bring in customers.

After she gave up her studio, Daphne went to people's homes to do family portraits, shot some photos in her own living room, and photographed some families outside. She still often photographs families outside, especially in the evening, "in the wonderful light we have in our country."

But she still needed to find creative ways to make herself known. The Strathcona County Chamber of Commerce ran an annual trade fair, and Daphne started going in 1994. The first year, she rented a booth and put up her pictures—"and it looked exactly the same" as the booths of the other five photographers. Daphne realized, "You can't look the same. You have to be different. You have to have something that stands out a little bit."

For the second trade fair, Daphne called on four friends with pretty little girls, built four "sets" and photographed each of the girls in front of each set. She displayed the photos at her booth, as well as one of the sets she had built as a backdrop for the photos. It was a hit. She sold a lot of gift certificates for people wanting their children photographed. After that, she developed a new theme for the booth each year.

Daphne had already been specializing in family and children's portraits. Then she discovered a coffee shop in the local mall which displayed local artwork. Daphne asked if she could display some of her children's portraits there, in the back area where local Moms came in for coffee in the morning. It turned out to be "a very good partnership." Fifteen years later, she is still getting business from that display.

Then Daphne found an even more memorable niche as "the angel lady." She made an agreement to erect a set in the window of a gift shop in the same mall shortly before Christmas. That is where she built her first "Angel" set. People could have their children photographed dressed as angels and surrounded by angels if they brought in a toy for the Christmas Bureau. After three years, the project had outgrown that location, and Daphne began taking photos in front of a fireplace in a heating and air conditioning store that also sold fireplaces. The effort provided good publicity for both the store and Daphne's studio. After five years of supporting the Christmas Bureau, Daphne switched to a different charity. Customers now make a $50 donation to A Safe Place, a women's shelter in Sherwood Park.

In the best year, Daphne did angel portraits for 720 families. She still does angel portraits every fall. "That is the one people come back for over and over and over again," Daphne says. "Children are the angels in our lives. All I do is help the parents see the wings."

The project made Daphne's business a success and allowed her to achieve her "absolute dream" of building a studio, attached to the house. "It was the angels who built my studio," she says. It is the ideal situation to have the studio so close and permanently set up, but still separate so Daphne and Art can "close the door on our business at the end of the day."

The annual angel project is still a significant part of Daphne's business. At first, she built a new angel set every year, although she is starting to reuse some older ones now. But she has also moved on to many other things. "I don't want to do just angel portraits."

Daphne recalls watching families come in with their daughters for angel portraits and telling their sons to sit in a corner and be quiet during the shoot. "Dads didn't want to see their little boys in a dress." So Daphne created "The Pond"—a set "with actual water where boys could play and fish and be silly." Girls also use The Pond, but Daphne has created a "Clubhouse" for boys, as well as other sets such as "Tea Party" and "Teddy Bears' Picnic" for both sexes. Each set is erected for a couple of weeks at a time in her studio, and an annual calendar tells customers when a specific set will be available. Designing the sets is an outlet for Daphne's creativity, and using a set over and over for a specific period of time is an efficient use of time. The traditional down time for photographers, the first three months of the year, are when Daphne does her planning and set designing. "I always have to be thinking of something new because my clients tend to come back over and over."

Carlyle Studio is now well established. Daphne does the marketing and the photography (except for large commercial jobs), and Art does the production. He is even developing a new line of "digital painting"—portraits done by computer graphics programs. The studio "went digital" in 2001 and produces its own prints instead of just sending negatives to a film lab. "There are so many more things we can do today. We can move people around and do whatever it takes so everyone looks great. That's the standard in the industry today. There is no more second best," Daphne says. "We are bringing in new technology all the time." Staying ahead requires constant effort. "We have to do things over, above, and beyond what the average person can do on Photoshop."

Daphne's work is much more than taking pictures. Her Web site (www.allaboutangels.net) states, "The mission of Carlyle Portraits is to create portraits that are beautiful works of art bringing joy to the hearts of their owners and all who view them. Pictures are what people look like; a portrait is who they are." In order to portray people as they are, Daphne has to first "build a relationship," something she is "pretty successful at." The goal is "to create a space for people to feel good about themselves."

Daphne has had many successes in her career, but she also sees her children and grandchildren as part of her success.

There have been difficult times in her life, but Daphne can't name any mistakes. "I don't think we make mistakes. We make choices and create situations for ourselves to learn something."

On how to find one's passion, Daphne suggests, "You have to know what you don't want before you can figure out what you do want. The Law of Attraction is my credo, my way of living—I believe we attract to us what we think about." Daphne's best advice is "Find your passion. Follow your dream. Find the one thing you want to do most of all and then do it. If you don't have anything that you care about, however big or small, you're not living."

Daphne adds, "You have to believe in yourself. When it comes right down to it, when you look in the mirror, that's the person who's responsible for everything in your life. You can't blame anyone else for where you are and what you're doing. And you have to learn to love yourself. I believe that very strongly. Here is an exercise I learned long ago from Arnold Patent, author of the book *You Can Have It All.* Go into the bathroom, look in the mirror, and tell that person you love her. Stay as long as it takes, even if you need to take a bag lunch in with you! By doing this, anyone can reach their full potential."

Making Things Work

Jessie Arlone Davies
Lawyer

If there is anything that characterizes Jessie Davies's life, it's an independent streak and dealing with life as it comes.

Jessie says, "I'm very independent. I always had to do things on my own. I didn't want to have to depend on anybody. I wasn't going to be somebody's wife. I was going to look after myself."

Jessie had a good relationship with her parents growing up—the models she learned the most from in her life. They are very hard working and have done very well. Her father is a grain farmer near Grande Prairie, Alberta, and her mother is a registered nurse. "But I usually like a challenge. I didn't want to do what they did, so I went my own way."

Jessie took her first two years of college in Grande Prairie, then went to the University of Lethbridge. She says, "I was eighteen. I went as far away as my money would take me at the time." When she got there, she needed to find a place to stay. Seeing a listing for shared accommodation, she immediately approached two other young students (one female and one male) and asked them if they would like to join her. This was a bit of a risk, Jessie says, since "I hate rejection." But the others "needed a place to stay as badly as I did." The three of them stayed together for the whole year. This was typical of Jessie and her penchant for "making things work."

Jessie isn't one to plan her whole life, but rather tends to move forward one step at a time, taking things as they come. "I've always been one to set a goal, reach it, and then say, 'now what?' Then I'll set another goal, reach it, and say, 'now what?' " She usually has a general plan, not a detailed one, and doesn't "do much thinking along the way."

Jessie doesn't remember what she wanted to be when she was younger. "But in high school, I wanted to be an accountant or a lawyer." So she did what she could and "kept taking the next step." She went to university, took accounting (earning a Bachelor of Management degree), got a job, and began to earn money. The job was with the CIBC bank. Starting right after graduation in 1992, Jessie worked in bank branches in Milk River, Mayerthorpe, Lethbridge, and Edmonton.

Jessie did well but became dissatisfied with her job. It was frustrating "to deal with clients and know that I could offer them more," she says. "I was tired of being just an order taker and wanted to offer more advice."

Jessie passed the Law School Admissions Test and enrolled in the Law School at the University of Alberta in 1998. Unlike most lawyers, Jessie had no one in her family who had been a lawyer. In fact, some family members wondered why she would want to go to law school when she already had a good career. They asked, "What more could you want?" It is typical of Jessie that she didn't listen but insisted on doing things her way. "Success for me is that I didn't let them keep me down. I wanted to be able to give more to people, and I wasn't sure that was necessarily going to happen where I was."

Jessie's decision was also "driven by money." She knew there would be considerable financial benefits to becoming a lawyer. At the bank, all there would be is a little more money each time she reached a new level.

Jessie is still grateful. The bank was very accommodating, allowing her to continue to work part time while she went to law school, so she didn't have to take student loans. The bank gave her flexible hours and allowed her to take extra time off at exam time.

Jessie graduated in 2001 and began articling at the law firm Duncan & Craig LLP, a very well-established law firm in Edmonton. She passed her licensing exams and was called to the bar a year later. She spent the next seven years as an associate at Duncan & Craig. "I don't bounce around," Jessie says, "I have staying power."

Jessie specializes in corporate, commercial, and banking law. Most of her clients are small corporations and businesses with one to five shareholders. She acts for them in dealing with banks and financial institutions and prepares documents such as partnership agreements, purchase and sale agreements, and non-competition agreements. She says a lot of her work is similar to providing insurance, providing a methodology ahead of time for resolving issues—how to get in and out of the partnership, how much each partner puts in, who's going to make the decisions, what to do if someone gets divorced or goes bankrupt.

"I enjoy the client contact very much," Jessie says, "having clients come in and say this is where we want to go, then helping them plan out on a legal basis what they need to do to get there"—whether this is seeing other experts such as a banker or an accountant, selling assets, or issuing shares. "Getting them from point A to point B is quite fun."

Jessie says, "I am also growing more comfortable in my career, figuring out what I need in order to make things work for me." Making things work is something she enjoys both in her career and in her personal life.

Still, Jessie's career change required considerable adjustment. There was "more flexibility," and she had to get accustomed to that. "I was still an employee, so I didn't have to worry about whether I was going to get paid," Jessie says. But she still had the pressure of meeting targets and getting her work done. "There are no set hours, you're a lawyer 24/7, and you do your work however and whenever you want to get it done ... Everything's left up to you. You have to set your own goals and plans." One thing Jessie doesn't enjoy is having to set out a detailed plan for her work on an annual basis. "I am more of a macro-level planner than a micro-level planner."

As a lawyer, Jessie is also responsible for keeping current in the law. "They tell us that right after you graduate, you actually know more law than someone who's further out," Jessie says. "You just don't have the application, the practical know-how of it." In law, you start as a generalist, "knowing lots about a lot of different areas," and gradually become more focused on one aspect of law, "leaving behind everything else you've learned." Keeping up in just one area of law is hard enough. "You have to take time to keep up—read legislative updates, join groups to discuss new issues, and talk to lawyers who practice in the same area of law."

Another thing Jessie didn't enjoy at first was networking—making contacts with other lawyers, and finding clients. "I'm a lot more familiar, more comfortable now with meeting people and finding out about them. I've learned to do that, and now I enjoy it quite a lot."

Jessie was married in 2001, a month and a half after she began articling. It was a difficult time, as her work was demanding. "I would get to work very early, between six and seven o'clock in the morning, and I would still be there at eight, nine, sometimes even ten in the evening. That was too much. I definitely don't do that anymore."

Her first child was born in 2004. She had "no structure or plan" for how to handle being a mother and a full-time lawyer. She took six months off and then went back to work. "I just dealt with it," she says.

Jessie's life became more complicated in other ways, too. She was diagnosed with multiple sclerosis in 2006, three months after her second child was born. She realized she'd had an earlier episode in 1998, but she is now in remission, not having had a relapse since. There are "visible signs that tell me it's still there," and it is "definitely linked to stress and how you are feeling," so she has to watch herself. "I make myself slow down. I make myself happier."

The challenges continue. Jessie is now trying to balance determining the next step in her career and her personal life, including raising her two children. She is at another "now what?" stage.

In the difficult times, Jessie remembers one of her mother's favorite sayings: "God doesn't give you more than you can handle." She adds, "You can always get through it, no matter what it is."

Jessie tends to be very reserved and not "get attached" to other people. "It scares me that someone might get to know something about me." But she has learned a lot from other people, often from observing them.

Jessie has also been ready to help others. In university and law school, she would often sit down with one or two other students and share her knowledge of courses. She found that by teaching, talking through issues with other people, she herself would learn more. The Canadian Bar Association also has a program which matches law students with practicing lawyers. When Jessie was a student, she learned a lot this way, and as a lawyer, she has mentored other students. Her experiences in this regard have been both good and bad. "When you're with a student who wants to learn, it's great." But one student, she says, was "much like me"—too independent—and didn't learn much.

Asked what mistakes she has made, Jessie doesn't point to any one mistake. "No matter what you set out to do, there are always setbacks. Some are big and some are small. Whatever happens, just be prepared to do your best."

Knowing what she knows now, there are some things Jessie would do differently. "I would likely still be taking the same path and setting the same major goals, but I would set minor, incremental goals as well, take a little more time. Everything was such a rush for me. I still have a habit of when I think I need something, I want it now. I would probably take more time and evaluate things a bit more. My intention is to plan more in this upcoming phase of my career and focus on my passion—my children and client interaction."

Jessie also says, "I am starting to share more." This means moderating her insistence on independence. "It is important to learn to accept support from those who will give it—and you may be surprised where it comes from." She adds that it is not hard to accept help but "it is sometimes hard to recognize that it's there ... Often we are in our own little world and think we can do this on our own." Sometimes support looks like interference. At such times, it is necessary to realize "the other person isn't there to get in your way, but to help."

On the other hand, Jessie is more convinced than ever that she has to take responsibility for her own life. She says, "To me, success is what you think it is, not what anyone else thinks it is. Some of the reactions you're going to get along the way aren't going to be supportive ... Sometimes you have to make decisions that shake other people's ground. It's not that you shouldn't give some reflection to the impact that you have on other people, but ultimately the only person responsible for you is you. Other people will shake your ground too, and you'll live through it."

Jessie is passionate about a lot of things—her children, her career, social clubs, participating in sports such as basketball, golf, and curling. She much prefers these activities to working out. "I'd rather exercise and not realize I'm exercising. When I'm playing basketball, I'm out there having fun."

Jessie hasn't thought a great deal about how people should go about finding their passion. Finding the things she is passionate about wasn't particularly difficult, but achieving her goals has taken a lot of hard work. She says that if people have a passion for something, they "will find a way to do it."

She advises, "If you are limited by resources, do what you can with the resources you have. You will gravitate toward what it is you want to do. Even if you are not one hundred percent sure of what it is, start doing something."

Her best advice is, "No matter what it is that you decide to do, be determined to do it. Know there are going to be setbacks, be prepared to work through them, and continue on with what you believe to be your path."

TEACHING THE LANGUAGE OF MONEY

Kim A. Deep

Founder and President, Kidz Make Cents

There were early indications as to what Kim Deep's passions would be (teaching, business, and accounting), but it took her a long time to put them together.

"I've always had a business," Kim says. At fourteen, she went to work in a nursery, but the work was hard and seasonal. So at fifteen, "I bought a small commercial caretaking business from a neighbor." It didn't take Kim long to realize that cleaning offices wasn't what she wanted to do either, but the business launched her into the world of entrepreneurship, helped her buy her first car at sixteen, and "was a source of income while I was going to school."

In time, she had two employees, and went to work at Kentucky Fried Chicken to learn more about business systemization and how franchises operate. This was a valuable experience in how to deliver quality customer service and run a business efficiently.

Her father was encouraging her to learn a profession and become a doctor, a lawyer, or an accountant, but seven or eight more years of school didn't appeal to her, so she enrolled in a two-year business administration course at NAIT (Northern Alberta Institute of Technology).

"I didn't seek out what I was passionate about. It wasn't a calling," Kim says. "I just went into things that seemed logical, that made sense." In her second year, she specialized in accounting, but not because she loved accounting. It was just that she was good with numbers, the course could lead to a professional certification, and accounting would be useful in growing a business. "It was practical."

Kim believes that her journey into the financial industry, although "unplanned" and "logical", was her subconsciously attempting to understand money issues that have always been a part of her extended family life. While growing up she saw siblings struggle financially and Kim says, "I was always intrigued by the dynamics and drama that money created in our family life." She had heard stories from her parents about them growing up with limited financial resources, and saw the scarcity and trauma that was always part of their siblings' lives. Money was a 'secret' that was never discussed openly but yet it was always there with drama and emotion, especially when 'there wasn't any'!"

With her newly developed business and money skills, Kim sold the caretaking business and began doing business and financial consulting. "I always had a business on the side," she says, "this was the best way for me to keep learning and growing my own financial skills. There is no better way to learn than the act of doing it!"

Kim chose to pursue a CMA (Certified Management Accountant) professional certification because she was more interested in the management side of business—working with people and systems, "taking the financial information and using it to make decisions." Kim says, "It was the people side of me."

While accountants are stereo-typed as being predictable and boring, that was never true of Kim. She jokes that in her case CMA stands for "Creative Management Accountant" since she has "a huge creative side." She paints, draws, does crafts, and writes poetry.

Kim still had no grand plan for her life, but she kept making logical decisions that moved her toward understanding money and business.

After graduating from NAIT, Kim worked for two years at the accounting firm Deloitte, Haskins and Sell (now Deloitte and Touche), learning and working with taxation issues for small business. Then she decided to learn how the economics of the business industry worked and found a job setting up financial systems for a company. The company became profitable, increasing its revenues from 2 to 6 million dollars in two years. Next, she decided she wanted to learn how government worked, so she found a job with the Alberta government doing statistical work monitoring spending.

In all of these moves, Kim says, "I was on a learning quest. My goal was to learn a diverse skill set, and ultimately, gain an understanding of finance and money."

By this time, Kim was married and pregnant with her first daughter. When she returned from maternity leave, she joined a private consulting firm, Financial Health Centre. Here, she helped small companies and professionals such as doctors and lawyers set up accounting systems and do financial planning. "I have a knack for doing clean-up," Kim says, noting that she often helped bring order to chaotic company records. Kim finds this ironic and somehow appropriate since her first business was a commercial cleaning company.

Next, Kim worked in the financial services department of the Edmonton Public School Board, where she set up a system to handle school-generated funds (for things such as field trips, textbook fees, fundraising) and tie them in to the schools' main financial systems.

After a year and a half, she had earned her CMA professional designation and became business manager for the school board's continuing education department. She also handled setting up the financial and technological systems for the newly opened Centre High, where students who hadn't finished high school in the regulation three years could complete their education and earn their diplomas. In two years, the budget she was responsible for expanded from 6 to 17 million dollars. She worked very long hours, reported to two bosses and found it "a huge learning experience." As difficult as it was, Kim says, "I was very passionate about the work I was doing." When her second child was born, she was in the middle of setting up a new software program for registration, so continued working part-time, taking her son to work. When her third child was born, she continued working full-time with her new daughter at her side, for eight months.

Looking back, Kim says, "I was working seventy hours a week, I loved the work I did, but I wasn't satisfied with what I was doing. I had no sense of fulfillment or purpose." She was in mid-career and still had not found her passion. Kim found herself in the midst of financial chaos and change with "not enough money" and "not enough time" always the mantras at work and at home. Her job was such a huge focus, controlling and monitoring spending on the business side, that Kim was not focusing on her own "Home Inc." business. Kim realized that she was following her parents' path of working harder, but she was not utilizing her financial skills for her own personal finances or sharing them with her kids. Her whole family had become afflicted with "affluenza" and they were not appreciating "the value of a dollar."

Consequently, in 2003, she entered "a path of self-discovery." She took some courses on business, money management, and personal development from Peak Potentials Training (www.peakpotentials.com) and hired a life coach to "help me find balance and harmony in my life." This led her to leave the school board in 2005.

Ironically, after years of part-time studying, years of learning on the job, nine years with the school board, and through her continued work with The Mastery of Self Expression (*www.themasteryworkshops.com*), Kim discovered a passion for teaching.

Kim clearly remembers "playing school" as a child. "I would line my brothers up in front of a chalkboard and make them do homework." Yet teaching never attracted her. At the school board, she taught secretaries how to use computerized accounting systems. She was able to "make it simple" so those without accounting training could understand. She was good at this, but not greatly enthused about it. "I discovered a skill, but not a passion." With Kim's down-to-earth approach to teaching money concepts to school board employees, and despite encouragement from her employer to teach some courses, "it just didn't appeal to me."

However, at Peak Potentials, she not only found direction for her life but "fell in love with the methodology." Peak Potentials' "accelerated learning strategies" were "more of a streetwise way of doing things, experiential learning," and she "realized that's how kids would be able to learn money concepts." This method of teaching, unlike anything she had encountered in school, appealed to Kim's creative side.

Kim also rediscovered a passion for writing and decided to write a children's book, *Conductor Kash and the Prosperity Express*, which was published in 2008. After attending a certification program in accelerated training, and experimenting with her financial concepts for kids, "I realized I could teach this." Essentially, Kim had decided to "take what I do and make it fun and engaging for kids." Kim's own unconscious quest to learn and understand the language of money was her training ground for her new-found mission.

Kim says, "Money is about facts—if your expenses are higher than your income, you're overspending." But "the creative aspect is the delivery model—how you teach and package the concepts." People are often "afraid of numbers," so it is important to take away the fear and the sense that handling money is a chore.

Part of Kim's motivation for beginning to teach financial management to children was the realization that no one was teaching this to her own children.

Kim's parents had never taught her about money other than teaching her by example to work hard. She and her husband, Darin, had been more affluent than her parents, but she realized that while they had been giving their children everything they wanted, what the children really needed was her time. She and her family were in "the affluenza mode"—bringing in and spending large amounts of money just because they could, without much thought as to why they were doing what they were doing. Kim says, "I began to wonder what type of legacy I wanted to leave my children." She realized that, rather than leaving them a monetary inheritance, which "won't amount to anything if you give it to them and they blow it," it was more important to leave them "the ability to create their own wealth." Kim also realized that what was true of her family was true of many others. Many children from wealthy families weren't handling money well because they had always had things given to them. Many children from poorer backgrounds weren't handling money well because they had never had much and had never learned how to earn it or put money to work for them. "Money is such a fundamental part of our daily lives, and no one was teaching how to manage it."

In 2006, Kim offered her first summer "Money Camp" to teach children ten and up how to handle money. She had already tried out some curriculum for younger children with pilot projects in daycare centers and playschools.

To help share her message of financial literacy and financial responsibility, Kim has developed an organization called Kidz Make Cents (www.kidzmakecents.com), and is launching The Family Wealth Academy in September 2009. She offers a week-long summer day camp, called Kidz Camp Millionaire, for ages ten to twelve. In schools and on weekends, the organization offers programs for every age range: Money Moolah (for children ages 3-4), Money Magnets (ages 5-6), Money Wizards (ages 7-9), Money Mania (ages 10-12) and Money Rules! (ages 13-17). She has a new initiative called Family Cents that supports families on their financial journey, and she offers a workshop called Money Matters for parents—because the parents realized they needed to learn what their children were learning.

Key to all the programs is teaching through games and activities and empowering families to take responsibility for their own choices about money. For instance, some of the programs use "money jars" to help the children put their money to work for them by assigning their money specific jobs/roles. They divide their money into portions for living expenses (needs), saving for financial freedom (investing), saving for contingencies and wants (such as vacations or automobiles), learning, fun, and sharing with others. When teaching is fun and engaging, Kim says, people remember it longer and can apply it better. Money is a language, she adds, and, like other languages, it is easier to learn it when you are young. Teenagers, on the other hand, can put the concepts into practice right away.

In spite of all of her professional accomplishments, Kim says her greatest success is her own three children, who are "great kids and very supportive." They are her inspiration for teaching other children.

Kim is enthused about what she is doing because "money really does make the world go around." But that does not mean that it is all about "the money." Kim is making money at what she is doing and says that her current work is fulfilling in ways that her earlier work was not. "Money is not the end but the means," she says. It is "a vehicle that can take you where you want to go." That being the case, Kim's teaching about money helps people "pick a vehicle that can get them there comfortably and in a timely fashion." Kim has chosen "the money train" as her vehicle and is passionate about it. She says, "I want to empower families to get on track with their finances and start enjoying the journey!"

What Kim teaches is not just about money but about tying money in with people's values. For instance, when people learn how to handle money well, they can focus not just on surviving (meeting basic needs such as food and clothing) but on thriving—and that often means being able to help other people. Kim's holistic approach to helping families manage money also gives parents resources to help facilitate health, happiness, and prosperity within the family unit and in their community.

One of the gratifying things for Kim is the profound implications of what she is teaching. Children who don't have financial stability often end up in crime and other problems. Therefore, teaching them how to handle money can turn their lives around. Taking responsibility for their own financial situation can be a starting point for taking responsibility for their lives and the choices they make on a daily basis.

Kim used to do a lot of volunteer work, and then got caught up in the rat race. Now she has been able to return to volunteering. In addition to her paid work, she does "pro bono" work, such as offering her teaching to YOUCAN, a program which helps youth at risk, and to the Centre for Family Literacy, an agency which offers literacy training for families and young children. She also does numerous school workshops every year to support her work with "Kids Kash in the Classroom"—an initiative to help inner school kids get a hand up and not a hand out in life.

Kim's business is rapidly expanding. In addition to her own programs, Kim appears as a regular on CBC radio with her column called Deep Pockets. She does frequent radio and TV interviews and writes regularly for *Island Parent* magazine and the Yummy Mummy Club. Kim also gives inspirational and engaging presentations for organizations and schools about success and living a life with purpose and passion. She has completed a second book, *The Prosperity Princess* and is a presenter with the Writers in School program sponsored by the Canadian Authors Association. Her product line of courses and teaching resources is continuing to expand, and she would eventually like to franchise her teaching around the world because the basic concepts apply in all cultures and would even work in a barter economy. Kim says, "ultimately what I teach about money isn't just about families and youth managing the tangible currency, but it's understanding the psychology and fundamental concepts and habits to become successful in all aspects of their lives.

Kim also has plans to create a program to help families and youth discover their passion. This would work together with the financial teaching, which helps them pursue and embrace their passion so they can live a purposeful life.

"My ultimate goal," Kim says, "is creating a foundation that helps people become financially independent." Called the FISH (Financial Independence Serving Humanity) Fund, it would go beyond offering immediate help such as a food bank gives. The goal would be to enable children and families to fulfill their dreams (have a book published or acquire capital to perfect an invention, for instance). Then, once they had become financially independent, they would be able to give back even more to the community and "make the world a better place."

It took Kim a long time to find her passion, but she suggests that some process is inevitable. "It is like trying on jackets until you find one that fits." She says that if she had had more direction around purpose and passion (such as she eventually found in Peak Potentials and The Mastery of Self Expression) when she was younger, it would have facilitated her journey. "Ultimately you get where you want to go, but it's great if there's some guidance, some people to help you get there a little faster."

If there is anything she would do over, it would be "to get out of my own way faster, to deal with my self-criticism and self-doubt a lot sooner." On the other hand, she has few regrets. "Everything I did was a learning experience." Even the experience of spending too much money got her to where she is now and has helped her to understand other people who are mismanaging money.

Kim sums up her best advice to others in three words:

- Focus: "Have a vision for what you want and where you want to go. It helps you focus on the destination and gives you a roadmap to follow. Without that, you will be paddling upstream, and it will be a very tiring journey."

- Attraction: "Believe in yourself, understand your values, know who you are, and expect opportunities to come your way, then you will look for them and know how to pick which ones you want."

- Action: "Take action on your vision, on what you believe in, every day. Pursue your passion with purpose, otherwise, it's not going to happen."

MAKING A DIFFERENCE

Faith Grant
Rejuvenation Health Services

From an early age, Faith Grant had a desire to make a difference in the world, to have an impact on those around her. Today, she has fulfilled that dream, leading a team of specialists who provide a holistic approach to health and wellness.

As a successful business owner, Faith has this advice to offer young entrepreneurs: discover what it is you really love to do and then do it! One way to tell if you are passionate about what you are planning to do is if your voice gets louder and louder as you are talking about it. An indicator that you may not be choosing what you really love to do is if people begin to yawn when you're talking about it!

Education and natural abilities are factors in making your choice to be a business owner but it is your passion that will give you the drive to succeed. Making your choice based on how much money you'll make is never a good idea, Faith says—you will soon get bored and work will become a chore.

Faith also suggests that young entrepreneurs seek out people who are successfully doing what they hope to do. Ask for their advice and learn from their mistakes—much better than having to make your own mistakes and learn from them! Educate yourself about businesses that are similar to your own. And remember, there will never be a "perfect time" to start a business. The most difficult thing is to start. Faith's advice is "just do it!"

Another thing that young entrepreneurs need to learn to do is become completely engaged with their clients. As Faith says, "They (the clients) must feel they are being heard, understood, and validated. No matter what business you embark upon, the key is to gain your clients' trust by showing them respect and by being humble. True humility has to do with looking outward, away from yourself; in this case, toward the needs of the client. When people come to consult you, 'they don't care how much you know; they want to know how much you care'" (from *The Purpose Driven Life* by Rick Warren).

There have been many influencers in her life, but Faith credits her elementary school teachers and her family as being those who have most helped her to achieve success. Even now, the names of her fourth grade teacher, Mrs. Henry, and her sixth grade teacher, Mrs. Townsend, come quickly to her lips as she recalls how they encouraged her to achieve excellence—a term Faith defines as "exceeding the highest expectation of others."

Her parents instilled in Faith the value of education. Though both very intelligent, work had taken priority over school when they were young and Faith's parents were determined to give their children the opportunity of the education they had been denied. A humorous story that Faith tells about her father is that he used to ride around the park to see if there were any children who were not in school. If he saw any, he would give them a ride to school on the back of his bike. Faith recalls the one day that she and her brother decided to skip school. They were so nervous about being caught by their father, they ended up going over to the high school and spending their time there. "It was no fun at all," Faith said. "We didn't do it again.'

Her parents also taught, by example, that a person should never limit themselves. Even though she had no training, Faith's mother was very talented musically and could teach her children songs in four-part harmony. Faith recalls, "I didn't ever feel restricted from doing anything. I could be what I wanted to be." Her mother's faith in God and her love for those around her helped Faith to view the world in a less self-centered way. The unconditional love she received from her Aunt Babs also had an influence on her. Faith says, "She was a good person whose life I wanted to emulate."

Wanting to help others was a strong motivating factor in her career choice and Faith has enjoyed being a physiotherapist for over twenty-five years now. But, she says, "I am not traditional in any way," and from early on, Faith could see that more was needed besides the traditional approach to health care services. She began to put together presentations that focused on wellness and empowering people to take control over their own health. Doing presentations in the Caribbean and for insurance companies and local businesses, helped to focus her attention on the need for a place where all the major players could be satisfied. Faith defines success as satisfied clients. These clients do not just include the person in need of care but also their family, their physician, and their insurance company. These other major players also need to be satisfied customers, confident that the health care given has been exceptional.

On November 4, 1992, when her second daughter was four months old, Faith decided to embark on the adventure of owning her own business. Having previously worked mainly as an independent contractor, Faith says, "I always wanted a sense of autonomy and some leeway with regards to how I deal with my clients. Even as a new graduate in Jamaica, I had private clients and on weekends I worked in a medical office as an independent physiotherapy provider. My last 'job' there was as a sole practitioner of a physiotherapy clinic in a private hospital. In 1992, I found that the place where I worked imposed too many restrictions and so off I went.

"We built a 'baby room' in a clinic in Edmonton, and my daughter came to work with me together with her babysitter. I was able to have the best of both worlds as the clinic developed. I could nurse her and see her all day. I was grateful that my older daughter was able to come to the clinic after school as well, so I didn't miss out on her telling me about her day."

A second clinic was started on January 3, 1994 and, as it turned out, that was a good decision. It is now the largest of their clinics and they decided to close the original one in December of 1995. Recently, they were approached by a national health and rehab company interested in discussing opportunities for partnership. They are now in partnership with them in their day-to-day operations.

In May of 2001, Faith says that she became restless and wanted to do something innovative. She decided to adopt a different approach, a more holistic one—and Rejvenation Health Services was born. They operated from two locations until recently (January of 2008) when they consolidated into one location in preparation for a major expansion in 2010.

Since 1994, Faith has owned and operated successful health centers, enjoying the autonomy and flexibility of entrepreneurship—and the ability to do *more*—to exceed people's expectations, to achieve excellence. Faith says that the multiple clinics have been due to her need to create. "I get bored when things are just clicking along and there is no longer any room to innovate."

At Rejuvenation Health Services, the staff works together as a team to treat the whole person. Included are: a physician, two physiotherapists, a dietician, two exercise therapists, a psychologist, two massage therapists and an acupuncturist.

Since it opened in 2001, the clinic has seen constant growth. They are adding new services and are planning a move to a larger facility in 2010. Faith's goal is that Rejuvenation Health Services will continue to expand as people come to see it as "the destination" for holistic health care.

Clients who have been to Rejuvenation Health Services are very fulsome in their praise using words such "highly recommend," "very pleased," and "impressed," citing the "knowledgeable, caring and friendly staff" who were "empathetic and respectful." And "most importantly, the treatment was effective and I felt great afterwards."

People come into the clinic for a variety of reasons. Some are referred by their doctor and some come on the advice of their insurance company. Often there is a primary concern such as, for example, knee pain. With the holistic approach at Rejuvenation Health Services, other things would also be investigated. Following the example of the person with knee pain, a physiotherapist might also look at what is happening to the hip joints as the person walks with the sore knee. There may be a need for foot orthotics. A dietician might be consulted if there is a weight problem that is contributing to, or resulting from, the injury. Consultations will be ongoing with the physician, who may see other contributing or resulting factors in the person's health such as high blood pressure or diabetes.

Faith says that since they opened in 2001, although services have been added and discarded according to space needs and the availability of qualified personnel, they have primarily been changed according to the feedback from their clients as to what services they most needed. Rejuvenation Health Services started off with physiotherapy and massage, but has since expanded to include: traditional Chinese medicine and acupuncture, weight management, anxiety and stress management, exercise therapy, personal training, foot orthotics, orthopedic shoes, non-surgical face lifts, and herbal products. They have recently added women's health services, which include treatment for: pelvic pain, urinary incontinence, painful intercourse, etc.

Botox, Pulsed Magnetic Field therapy, and Acupuncture facelift treatments are available as non-surgical options. Help is also available for those who would like to quit smoking or lose weight through nutrition counseling, anxiety and stress management, and empowerment through education.

Always the client is empowered through education to take control of their own health. Support from family, coworkers, and their physician is important but recovery will depend primarily on the client. They are the ones who will have the greatest impact on their own wellness. As Faith says, "We are consultants, educators—a small part of the whole process."

A line of products is available from Rejuvenation Health Services. "Relief" is an odorless, non-staining comfort rub for relief of muscle and joint aches, strains and sprains, tendonitis, and even TMJ discomfort. "Regrow" is an exclusive hair restoration lotion, which has been used successfully in the U.K. for over ten years. Formulated with moisturizers and emollients, "Regrow" has been shown to stimulate hair growth in cases of premature baldness and hair loss due to illness, stress, or disease.

Their product line, registered under the label, "HealthSmart," consists of better than cosmetic-grade moisturizers. For example, the lotion they carry can be used by anyone with sensitive skin, even eczema, and will yield at least 6:1 as compared to an off-the-shelf lotion of the same volume. Rejuvenation Health Services is currently looking into doing research to document their results.

What makes the clinic and its products unique is that it is a one-stop shop: whatever problem someone might be experiencing, they have a product or service to address it. As Faith says, "We treat our clients as partners and we engage them fully in order for us to understand their needs and to actually meet them."

Gift certificates are available in any denomination and can be purchased for any of the services provided by the clinic.

Therapeutic exercises and personal fitness are also provided by Rejuvenation Health Services. And Faith and the staff show, by example, healthy life choices—some of them bike or walk to work even in inclement weather. Faith feels that her staff is fully engaged with her mission and vision. "They really have heart. People feel the staff is there for them."

Faith says that over the years, she has learned how to "roll with the punches" because as an entrepreneur, you cannot avoid these. "I discovered how to absorb the energy from them and use it as a propellant for my next move. I also learned that I will make mistakes, but as long as I feel that a valuable lesson was gained, then nothing I do can be in vain. Finally, but not lastly, I have learned that I can't do it alone. I have come to rely on a higher power for guidance, direction, approval, pre-approval, and justification. Basically, if what I do pleases God, then it can't be bad for other people."

Faith's husband is also supportive of the work that Faith does. "He helps me to be more confident," she says, admitting that she is naturally a shy and reserved person. "My husband helps me to be a stronger person." Faith also says that her two daughters have helped her to mature. Her older, more practical daughter and her younger, "huggy" daughter have, each in their own way, helped her gain more practical and more emotional maturity. Faith says of raising her daughters that she prays that she will be a good influence on them—that they also will seek excellence in all they do, each in their own unique way.

Faith and her daughters enjoy Tae Kwon Do and Faith has earned her black belt. Her personal goal for 2009 is to train for the World Masters Games, which are held every four years (similar to the Olympics). In October of 2009, they will be held in Sydney, Australia, and Faith is hoping to compete in running the 400-meter race.

Besides continued expansion of Rejuvenation Health Services, Faith says that the next phase of her life might involve education or corporate consulting. Originally from Jamaica, she is also considering ideas for the Caribbean that are not necessarily in her field, for example, a Vegan resort. But whatever she does in the future, making a difference will still be Faith's goal. "I want to feel I have made an impact. That people will feel like a good wind went by. That they are better for it."

LOOK AND FEEL GREAT

Deborah Kurach
Verve Salon and Spa Ltd.

Appearance may not be everything, but in the beauty industry it counts for a lot—just ask some of Deborah Kurach's satisfied guests at Verve Salon and Spa.

The little black dress 44-year-old Kelsey Logan wore to dinner in Paris last Christmas was a triumph. The dress was sleeveless—a style she hadn't worn in more than twenty-five years. In the past, she would have been too embarrassed by the unseemly scars running down her left arm. The trail of scars was also a painful reminder of months of abuse Kelsey had endured at the hand of an abductor years ago. Thanks to the work of Deborah Kurach at Verve Salon and Spa, Kelsey's life and looks were transformed forever.

The spa, one of the most beautiful in the area, is located in Alberta's Sherwood Park, just east of Edmonton. Guests enjoy a full array of spa services. One of those services is permanent make-up and Laser treatments, a specialty of owner/operator Deborah Kurach.

Deborah says one of her career highlights, since opening the successful spa and salon in 2001, is the effect her work has on the lives of people like Kelsey. "That was one of the most touching

71

things I've done." Thanks to a half dozen laser treatments and the application of skin-toned camouflage mineral make-up, the scars on Kelsey's arm have been significantly reduced and covered up.

"I've lived with the stigma all my life," says Kelsey, who now lives in Edmonton. "When my husband, Colin, and I first found out Deborah was even going to do the treatment, we actually cried ... then I bought my first little black dress ... and wore it in Paris this past December." Having the treatment "gave me the confidence to do it," says a beaming Kelsey.

Helping people feel good about themselves and their appearance is a big part of what drives the energetic team of fifty staff at Verve Salon and Spa.

Having spent many years in the beauty industry, Deborah says, people's attention to body image has changed. "In our industry, people want to look their best ... I think now more than ever, people are more aware of taking care of themselves, being healthy, and doing things that are right."

Of course appearance plays a large role in our society, whether it's through the influence of magazines, billboards, or other advertisements. But it's mostly personal, Deborah says, "and has to do with getting things right in your head." Looking good on the outside simply helps people feel better about life in general. It increases their sense of well-being and adds to their level of calm. Taken together, all of this helps people cope better with life and even make better decisions. Overall, looking your best can play a vital role in living a successful life. "If your appearance is there, then people respond to you differently. They have more respect for you if you look your best."

Today, "Verve is everything I want my business to be," says Deborah, from her well-appointed and fashionable salon done up in lime green, taupe, plum, and terra-cotta tones. "VERVE means Vivacious, Energetic, Resilient, Vibrant, and Enthusiastic," she says, referring to the acronym for the business that she and her husband, Lynn, run together.

When people leave the calming spa, they say things like, "I wish I didn't have to leave," or "I feel like I've been on a holiday," or "I wish I could stay here forever," Deborah confides.

With the easy access from the parking lot and the central location on Athabascan Avenue, people begin to unwind the moment they walk through the doors. From the stylish brushed steel reception desk, to the scented rooms and intimate tables, the spa is meant especially to soothe and rejuvenate body and mind. In the spa, "the music is relaxing and puts people in a different state of mind."

Ashley Svitich, who has worked at the reception desk at Verve for the past six months, enjoys the friendly, upbeat, rejuvenating atmosphere and its effect on guests. "I love to greet people and you can tell they've enjoyed their time," says Ashley. "They're very relaxed."

Obviously the spa, with its full line of products and tools to complement the work of the well-trained staff, offers people a getaway from the everyday rush and hassles of life. But behind the scenes, creating such an oasis of tranquility requires a lot of hard-nosed attention to detail.

"We have a very professional look ... our STAFF are spirited, talented, active, fresh, and have a lot of freedom," she adds, easily slipping in another acronym. When she hires staff, she looks for people who present themselves well and will put others at ease. This attention to detail is one of her strengths.

Deborah, who was born in Wilke, Saskatchewan, spent about ten years in sales and education in the beauty industry before deciding she wanted to open her own business in her adopted hometown of Sherwood Park. She wanted her business to be a one-stop shop, offering a wide range of products to staff and guests alike.

The list of services is long. Specializing in laser hair reduction, skin firming, rejuvenation, and scar diminishing treatments, Verve Salon and Spa also offers pregnancy massage (beds come complete with openings for belly and breasts), facials, sports and French manicures, pedicures, skin care (promising detoxification and de-stressing benefits), waxing, sunless tanning, makeover applications, customized bridal packages, and permanent make-up options.

Invitingly, Verve Salon and Spa also offers couple packages that treat you to a tub soak and body scrub in addition to a healthy lunch, manicure, pedicure, facial, and massage. It all sounds good, but it's not necessarily easy. Lots of people want to open their own salon, says the successful entrepreneur, but it means showing up for work and generally maintaining an old-fashioned, everyday work ethic. "I'm the type of person who never missed a day of work, or a day of school," she says.

She adds that staying focused is important. The business is her primary concern. Fortunately, this successful woman does not currently struggle with work/life balance.

It also means doing your research, educating yourself, and sometimes just staying the course. "If I didn't know what I was doing, I'd have changed the skin and body care lines about twenty-five times," she laughs. But Deborah did her research before opening the salon and selected a quality line out of Sweden that is distributed in Canada. Of course the hair salon aspect of the business is different and requires constant upgrades. Keeping up with styles, such as the latest in colored hair extensions or colored nail tips for gel nails, and technolo-gies is a big part of the equation.

Deborah also learned a lot from her sister, Carolyn, who worked as a stylist for thirty years in Saskatoon. "My sister was a big influence," says Deborah. "Her passion for what she was doing ... she loves the guests, she loves hearing their stories."

Working with others, including her husband, Lynn, sister, Melinda (manager of Verve Operations), daughter, Connie (cur-rently one of Verve's front-end receptionists), and Tammy (a Master Hair Stylist) makes it all worthwhile. "These relation-ships are important," says Deborah.

Figuring out your own passion and being willing to share your knowledge and skills with others, is a big part of what it takes to be successful, says the Alberta businesswoman. "If I had it to do over, I'd pray to recognize my best talents sooner," she says. "The more you share and assign and have others do things for you and with you, the better. You can't do it by yourself."

"I feel anyone can be successful—man or woman. I do feel women have to work hard ... I do believe in women being strong leaders, especially in this industry."

This business also gives back. The salon contributes to community projects on a regular basis. Professionally, Deborah and the management team continually invest in their own staff, who wear monogrammed and, recently, sequined black aprons and slacks. Verve promotes training opportunities, entering contests, and provides the latest in products and tools.

Each year, the entire staff receives a makeover for an annual photo shoot (check out their gorgeous Web site at www.vervesalon.ca). This year their makeover theme will be Barbies, complete with sets and make-up. The fun-loving nature of the staff only enhances their profession, when you consider their job is to make people look and feel their best.

In keeping with the spirit of congeniality and professionalism, Deborah explains the point of entering contests is not to win, but to constantly strive toward doing and being your best. Of course, Deborah easily admits to her own competitive nature and her desire to be her best at all times.

She is also a risk-taker. "If I wasn't a risk-taker, I wouldn't be doing what I'm doing," she says. "You definitely learn and grow from your mistakes." Don't be afraid to make a mistake, advises the seasoned businesswoman.

Some of the bigger lessons she has learned along the way are financial—such as don't pay for materials prior to delivery. And others "you only learn with age," she reflects. Regardless, if you want to be a success, "you have to be a risk-taker."

And how do you recognize success when you've achieved it? Deborah counts among her successes: good relationships, a growing business that has been in operation since 2001, a loyal staff, and happy, satisfied guests.

Perhaps the greatest marker of success is that every day someone new walks through the doors and enters the calming, transformative atmosphere that is Verve Salon and Spa. Most of the clientele are repeat customers, but other people are still hearing of the spa through word of mouth and advertising. Keeping an eye on growth and expansion is very important to running a successful business, says Deborah.

Currently, about 20 percent of her clientele are men, while 70 percent of her guests are women. Many bring their children or grandchildren to enjoy the calming experience of a first-time manicure or pedicure, or even a stylish haircut. Children account for about 10 percent of the business.

"They never forget it," says Deborah of the young children in the stylist or technician's chair. Many bring their friends for a birthday party and most of them are sure to come again. "They like the hand cream we use for them. You can see it in their face. They love it." Lots of mothers and daughters make Verve their special outing together.

If success is doing what you enjoy and in the process bring fulfillment to others, as Deborah says is her own definition of the elusive term, then she seems to be doing a lot of things right. She has passion; she has drive; and she works to enhance the lives of others. "Do what you like to do," she advises. "That is what gives you the drive to work on your goals."

It's a good thing she's willing to share in the good work because reaching her goals means a lot of others are able to reach theirs—to look and feel their best after a trip to Verve Salon and Spa.

A COMMON THREAD OF
DOING BUSINESS

Carmen LaFrance
Owner, Southern Alberta Womanition Magazine

Little did Carmen LaFrance know, as a middle child with twelve siblings, how significant it would be to learn to be a true team player. This knowledge has served her well in the past year as she has worked with Womanition co-owners, Angela Sladen and Dorothy Briggs, to develop the Womanition franchise for southern Alberta. The year 2008 was a year of celebrating successes and overcoming challenges, including a severe case of vertigo.

Asked who has been the most influential person in her life, Carmen is quick to respond that all of the members of her family have, in some way, contributed to her success today.

Carmen's Grandmother and Grandfather LaFrance were early pioneers and self-made business owners. In the late 1940s, Carmen's grandfather owned one of the first combines and a three-ton truck, and contracted out his services to American farmers to harvest their crops. He would start down in Kansas and work his way up through Montana, following the harvests north, back home to Alberta. That was when he learned that having your own business sometimes requires making agonizing decisions. On one of these trips, his son-in-law died of a sudden illness. Carmen's grandfather had the body sent home by train but had contracts to fulfill and couldn't get home himself in time for the funeral. Carmen's grandmother was a business woman in her own right. She made the best butter in town—and was proud of every pound of butter sold bearing the stamp "LaFrance butter."

Both Carmen's mother and grandmother were responsible to "hold down the fort" when their respective husbands were gone for months either to Kansas or working in the wood mill in the wintertime. These courageous, ordinary women worked very hard to plow the way to accomplish extraordinary things.

Carmen will also forever cherish fond memories of her Grandfather Fontaine, who lived a very simple life, modeling his philosophy of contentment into his early nineties. She remembers the small, one-room shack he lived in during the summer. "There was just a bed and a table in there—he lived very simply—but he was widely known for his amazing garden and for his contagious smile that brought joy to everyone around him. He modeled the truth that 'Happiness is a journey not a destination.'"

Carmen loved to be her dad's "right-hand person," and not much deterred this tiny five-foot-nothing from operating large machinery or moving herds of cattle with her horse and blue heeler dog. She always gave 110 percent in all she did, even picking rocks. She only learned on her Dad's recent eightieth birthday that it was a leap of faith and a determination to follow his heart that transformed the LaFrance farm from poverty to prosperity. In the mid-1970s, Mr. LaFrance, along with his wife, Marie, and his right-hand person, Carmen, set out for a six-hour drive, pulling a borrowed tent trailer, to attend a full-blood Limousin sale south of Calgary. Hotels were not an option for the LaFrance family in those days. On his eightieth birthday, Mr. LaFrance shared with Carmen how terrified he was of bidding for his dream cow, because he had no idea how he would pay for it. Seventy-three thousand dollars and a few years later, Mr. LaFrance became well known for his amazing Limousin herd.

One year, their family swept up all the annual 4-H trophies!

It was Carmen's sisters, Lucie and Colette, who were instrumental in helping her overcome her fear of public speaking. As a young girl in 4-H, she was required to make an impromptu one-minute speech. Her topic was "How to Make Money." Carmen recalls how shy she was and how difficult it was for her to talk in public. When her sisters started to laugh at her, Carmen burst into tears. Later, at home, she cried herself to sleep and promised herself that she would never speak in public again. The next day, however, was a brand new day, and as she was feeding the cows, she thought, "The heck with them! They won't deny me the opportunity to develop myself!" Young Carmen then began to prepare a speech about "Pollution in the Year 2000" and won the first-place trophy! For her, this was a big stepping-stone and made her determined to never give up.

Carmen's parents gave their children opportunities to cultivate their gifts, and today most of Carmen's siblings are in business or have been in business. Now that her own daughters are grown and successful in their careers, Carmen says, "I've decided to become an entrepreneur at the ripe young age of fifty. It's never too late to start new projects."

It was the "law of attraction" that first started Carmen in a new business. "For me, 2008 was a blissful, eventful year, and I started with Womanition because I was vibrating at that level. I had been talking and thinking about owning my own business, and lo and behold a little blonde angel named Dorothy phoned me up one day and offered me the opportunity to purchase a Womanition franchise."

What attracted her to Womanition, Carmen says, was a passion she shared with the other Womanition leaders for supporting women and children in need. She also embraces the purpose of Womanition, which is to create an avenue of support for women in business. "I saw a need for a professional magazine that would promote brilliant, successful business women."

Carmen launched the Calgary and Red Deer (southern Alberta) *Womanition* magazine in 2008. In 2009, she formed a partnership with Ronda Bertram, who had bought the franchise for Fort McMurray. Both women now co-own both franchises. Carmen describes Ronda as "an incredibly savvy business woman with a heart of gold." She adds, "From day one, I have admired Ronda for her authenticity, integrity, and resilience, and for knowing when to make those difficult business decisions." Carmen says she and Ronda "are truly passionate" about helping entrepreneurial women grow their businesses, and joining their skills and resources has increased their ability to do that (see www.rondabertram.com).

For Carmen, success is keeping the wheel of harmony in balance. Some things needing to be kept in balance are health, giving and receiving, time and money. "Money is nice, but it is certainly not the 'be all, end all' many people believe it to be. Keeping the wheel of harmony balanced is pivotal to being successful in both your personal and business life."

Carmen also believes that success is leaving a legacy that will have a lasting impact on people, whether it is being a pillar in your community, doing humanitarian work at home and abroad, or simply being a role model for those around you. She says, "Just touch someone's life. As Mother Teresa said, 'If you can't feed one hundred people, just feed one.'" This way of living has its own rewards. "If you help bring joy to the life of another person, it comes back to you a hundred-fold." Carmen says that if she won a million dollars tomorrow, not much would change in her life, as she is a happy and contented woman. She would invest the money wisely and share with those less fortunate, helping them to discover and develop their gifts, talents, and skills.

The profound messages of both Eckhart Tolle, author of The Power of Now, and Elisabeth Fayt, author of Paving it Forward (www.elisabethfayt.com), have had a huge influence on

Carmen's life. Today, she lives life more in the moment of now, as "we never know what tomorrow will bring. We should not aimlessly dash through life not stopping to smell the roses. We should celebrate life and not take it for granted."

Carmen also believes that in order to be open to changes and embrace the concept of excellence, one must first have an open mind. "The mind is like a parachute; it works better when it is open. Life and business are forever evolving; therefore, it is imperative that we be open to change. I love change. For me, it's about learning new perspectives, being flexible, and adapting to the unknown. Embracing the concept of excellence is a must in my business and my personal life. I didn't say 'perfection' because there is no such thing. But you can only achieve what you aim for, so aim high." Carmen has learned that when people are clear on their business intentions, the help, learning, and opportunities they need readily present themselves.

She also believes that one of the core foundations to success is building strong, healthy relationships. "A network of great connections is worth a million bucks." To create healthy relationships, it is first necessary to be well connected to yourself. Knowledge found in textbooks is great, but knowing yourself is where it all needs to start. After that, it is possible to learn from others. Carmen says, "There is no need to reinvent the wheel. There are many successful entrepreneurs and business owners from all walks of life from whom we can learn. Follow in their footsteps, and then add your own creative juices and spices to give your business its own unique flavor. Your personal touch can be as spicy or creative as you wish."

For Carmen, passion is a key factor in the equation of success. "Passion is what creates the drive and determination when the going gets rough." To discover your passion, she advises that you listen in the stillness for an "ah-ha moment." You will know it is authentic when you feel a yearning to do it, no matter what.

In spite of all the obstacles, you will reignite it, get the wheels turning, and never settle for mediocrity.

We seldom think of the larger purpose when we are young, Carmen says, but after being a student in the "school of life " for a few decades, we can see the larger purpose more clearly. She has many passions and "would have to live a thousand years to experience them all." She enjoys yoga, dancing, remembering her roots, connecting with nature—and she is determined to learn how to swim before her departure from Mother Earth. But two passions in particular are close to her heart. One is empowering and supporting women and children locally and abroad. "Something beyond words happens in your heart when you help someone move from poverty to self-sustainment to prosperity—and give them a chance in life. I am so proud to be a part of a powerful new model for business and humanitarian living called HUB (Humanity Unites Brilliance, www.carmen.hubhub.org). What if you could support yourself and the world at the same time—while experiencing your passion and making a difference? There is no limit to the positive impact we can create together when we unite our brilliance for the greater good."

Another passion is the environment. As Carmen is fast approaching her retirement from Canada Post, she has taken the initiative to recycle the plastic packaging in her section. "If people only knew how many years it takes to decompose plastic, they would not hesitate to take the easy steps to recycling," she says. "Recycling is a win-win proposition." Although she is "not in a position to pull the strings to implement a system, I still am doing what I can at this moment." She believes it is very important to have respect for Mother Earth and to be careful to not destroy ourselves. "We should not take for granted what God has given us. We need to be innovative and accountable so we do not steal from future generations." Carmen says that it was her two daughters, Nicole and Sarah, who first helped her to recognize the need for recycling.

Carmen also credits her two girls with being a big influence in her life in other ways. Carmen recalls telling her young daughters that they would teach their mom and dad about life. The girls could not imagine how that could be possible. But many years later, when her daughter Sarah was fourteen, she was able to help her mom "face the music" with regards to the decision to separate from her husband. Carmen says, "I learn so much from them as a parent. I have learned that these children of ours are only on loan to us for a brief moment. It is our responsibility to teach them and give them the necessary wings they need to fly." She adds, "My mother, two daughters, and eight sisters are the most important women in my life. The mother/daughter/sister relationships that I treasure are all about bringing the best out of each other and supporting each other's passions. My mother, daughters, and sisters have taught me so much about life, but one thing I would like to share is: Think twice and speak once; then you will have no regrets." Carmen's mother was diagnosed with breast cancer last year, and one of her grandest wishes is to experience a fishing trip with her nine daughters. That wish will come true in July 2009.

Carmen says that fear has been one of the biggest challenges she has had to overcome. "Operating out of fear denies you the delightful opportunity of playing outside the box and discovering your potential. You need a strong backbone to be in business," she says. "I've learned to embrace my fears. Life is not about how to survive the storm but about how to dance in the rain. It is not a failure when you have learned something from the experience. We need to experience the valleys in order to appreciate the mountains. And, as Einstein said, 'Within every adversity resides a glorious opportunity.'"

Carmen believes that there is no simple magic formula for success. You need a visionary plan with effective, efficient systems in order to operate a successful business. She is also very grateful for her fabulous Virtual Assistant, Sharon Price (sapcalgary@shaw.ca).

Carmen says, "By far, my proudest business success was the launching of *Womanition South* magazine in 2008." Her greatest personal success in life, so far, has been to successfully "teach my daughters to soar like eagles."

If she had it all to do over again, she says, "I would start life at twenty with the knowledge, confidence, wisdom, and experience I have today at fifty. Sometimes we just need to get out of our own way and allow life to unfold."

There is a common thread that runs through Carmen's life, through the lives of her ancestors, and hopefully through the lives of future generations. Like her parents and grandparents, Carmen has stepped out of the box, has moved into "the uncomfortable zone", has taken a risk, and is following her heart.

For Carmen LaFrance, embracing life is what it is all about.

"Keep your glass half full at all times."

SAFETY, FEAR, AND GRATITUDE

Barbara Lynn Semeniuk
Owner, Purcell Enterprises Ltd.

Barbara Lynn Semeniuk is a highly regarded occupational health and safety expert who owns her own company. Asked how she got into her current career, Barbara Semeniuk gives a short answer: "Serendipity."

Barb didn't set out to be an entrepreneur. She earned a Bachelor of Science degree in biology from Simon Fraser University in 1983 and became a research assistant in a tuberculosis laboratory. But a spill of the TB virus in the lab caused her to become interested in worker safety. (Although no one was harmed, the spill was serious since the TB virus can live up to six to eight months outside the human body.) Barb ended up writing an academic paper about the TB virus, with encouragement and assistance from her boss, Dr. Judy Isaac-Renton. The incident also motivated her to earn an Occupational Health and Safety Diploma from British Columbia Institute of Technology in 1988.

That pushed her into the health and safety field. It was a difficult time. Barb was recovering from a bad first marriage and trying to make it in a new field that was largely dominated by men. She worked first as a district health and safety officer for

Haliburton Services Ltd., a multinational petroleum company. Her work involved inspecting sites and giving safety seminars. Then she worked as a consultant for what is now Enform, the training, certification, and health and safety services arm of the upstream petroleum industry.

Next she worked as a technical advisor for the Alberta Construction Safety Association. For four years, she was responsible for standards such as WHMIS (Workplace Hazardous Materials Information System) and TDG (Transportation of Dangerous Goods), which require that workers be informed of the dangers they are working with. A "globally harmonized" version of WHMIS is coming out shortly, which will prescribe the same standards for every country of the world.

After that, a consultant had her doing audits for the Alberta Motor Transport Association, and then she became occupational health and safety coordinator for Edmonton Public Schools.

Finally, in 1997, Barb started her own company, Purcell Enterprises Ltd., which offers safety audits and safety training to other companies in a variety of fields, including the trucking, construction, food processing, manufacturing, oilfield, retail, and security industries. The main reason for striking out on her own, she says, is "the Plexiglas ceiling"—she repeatedly got passed over for promotions, and it was difficult to get ahead in companies dominated by men. "I suck at office politics," she says. Running her own company, she doesn't have the same kind of frustrations. "I like the freedom to set direction, and the harder I work, the more money I make." It also gives her the opportunity to choose her clients, to "work with people I like."

Again the transition was difficult. Barb was going through her second divorce, and now had a daughter to raise. It took three years to build up a clientele and get her company established.

LESSONS ALONG THE WAY

Along the way, Barb has learned a number of lessons. One is to not quit. In the most difficult transitions in her life, she has had to "pick myself up" and start something new. She has also had her share of conflict. "Opposition just drives me to do it."

If she had it all to do over again, Barb says, "I would have tried to have less fear." As one of the first women to work as a consultant for the Alberta Motor Transport Association, she remembers driving alone through the wilderness in her F-150 pickup truck, following unmarked "lease roads," counting kilometers and looking for small signs that would show her how to get to the oil rigs she was supposed to be checking on. Her territory covered everywhere from Slave Lake and Whitecourt to Edmonton and Lloydminster, yet she managed to find her way.

Barb also experienced great anxiety about teaching, always afraid that she would not do well—even though she did. She taught seminars for the Alberta Construction Safety Association until 2007 and for Alberta Food Processors, and has taught at Red Deer College and Lakeland College. "The only difference between a beginner speaker and an expert speaker," she quips, "is that the expert speaker's butterflies fly in formation."

Another lesson is the importance of "working on your business as well as in it." Barb enjoys the day-to-day, hands-on work. "I'm not big on long-range strategic planning. I never had a business plan when I started my company. I'm big on being flexible." But she says that in any business it is necessary to do strategic planning and analyze strengths and weaknesses, opportunities and trends.

Part of that work includes staying current. Barb reads a lot, most of it non-fiction. "I strive to educate myself and be in the forefront of my field." Doing safety audits under eight different standards in three provinces requires "continuous learning."

Barb succeeds because she "loves a challenge" and "doesn't like being bored."

That love of a challenge also feeds into another of Barb's passions—shopping. She says, "I love the hunt, the challenge," especially looking for things that others can't find. She recalls the time she found a red shower curtain for her sister-in-law.

Barb gained some of her love of learning from her parents, who expected her and her brother and sister to go to university. Even though he had only grade three education when he came to Canada as a sheepherder from Yugoslavia, her father taught himself to read English. He believed strongly in education and was "one of the smartest men I knew." Barb also remembers Miss Auld, a French teacher who developed Barb's love of travel and her desire to learn through travel.

Another lesson is the importance of "delivering value." As an entrepreneur, she says, "You have to be responsive to your clients' needs, but you don't pander to them. Clients are not always right, sometimes you have to take them to the next level, and sometimes you have to correct them."

In her second year of owning her own business, even though it was not yet well established, Barb says she began to "fire clients," particularly those not interested in safety. As an entrepreneur, "you are a reflection of your clients." Barb's clients have included many well-known multinational corporations, including Costco, Save-On Foods, Wendy's, BFI, Canadian Waste, Syncrude, Mobil Oil, and Jomax Drilling. Good clients "drive you to do better."

Bad clients, however, refuse to be helped, and that presents a poor picture of those trying to help them. Barb remembers one businessman who struck her as "evil" and "a sociopath." At first, he seemed very committed to safety. Later, he told her that he had discovered very few people get fined for safety violations and added, "I don't care if I kill someone." The man had built a fortune on the backs of his workers and others. Barb told him she couldn't work with him. She also told a government inspector to "throw the book at him."

Barb did an audit at another company where the employees all described the owner as "an idiot who treated them like dirt." Her report pointed out that morale among the company's employees was poor and that the company would go bankrupt if changes were not made.

Barb has learned that if workers are treated badly, they will either leave or do bad work. Therefore, companies should treat their employees well "from pure self-interest," if for no other reason.

In contrast, Barb admires an owner who practices the "Alexander principle." It was said of Alexander the Great that he would not demand of his soldiers anything that he was not willing to do himself.

Barb herself has had some very good bosses and some very bad ones. "A lot of people who reach very high positions are sociopaths who walk on the bodies of other people." She is determined to "be the boss I've always wanted to have." She doesn't actually have employees but uses sub-contractors. For instance, she gets help from a 72-year-old lady who "can make my computer sing." She adds, "We work very well together, she's very innovative, and she doesn't put up with any nonsense."

Barb has also used another sub-contractor to do audits. He does a great job, so Barb paid him 700 dollars a day instead of the 500 dollars he asked for. As a boss, Barb is free to pay people what they are worth.

Those relationships demonstrate Barb's ability to work with both men and women. Even in biology, she says, the field was 60 percent men. "I've always enjoyed the company of men," she says, and men are very direct, an approach she prefers. If road builders didn't like what she was telling them, they would "tell me to fart off." School principals, on the other hand, would smile and be nice to her to her face and then complain about her to her bosses. (In their defense, Barb says the school principals had enormous workloads, and health and safety issues were just one more thing they were responsible for.)

Another lesson, Barb says, is that "you have to give back." She cites a proverb from her Anglican background: "Cast your bread upon the water, and you'll receive back manyfold." It is something her parents taught and exemplified. In plain language, it means, "the more you help others, the more successful you become." Barb has given free safety training to Bosco Homes (a social service agency that helps adolescents in crisis), and also contributes to cancer research and the Foster Parents Plan.

Barb also says, "I am a big believer in tolerance and diversity", which she learned from her parents and which she sees as "a foundation for community." She cites the golden rule, "Treat others the way you would like to be treated," and the proverb, "Leave a place better than when you got there."

Another lesson Barb has learned is the importance of a sense of humor. She recalls a time when her daughter was in grade six and stepped on a safety association binder Barb had left on the floor of her office. One of the rings penetrated her daughter's toe, and they couldn't get it out. After paramedics transported her to the hospital, she told all the doctors and nurses, "My mother is a safety person."

Barb has a highly successful career and has done over a thousand safety audits, but she says her greatest success is raising her daughter, Dianne, who is a good and brilliant person. When her daughter was taken to the hospital, she discovered that the paramedics keep a supply of stuffed animals to give to the children they transport. As a result, Dianne organized twelve friends and collected over 500 stuffed animals for the ambulance service.

Barb and her husband shared custody of their daughter, caring for her alternating weeks, something which was "quite innovative in the 1990s." She believes that "a child needs both parents," and she and her husband were careful not to criticize each other to their daughter. Barb says it is important that a parent remain a parent, not a friend, and set values and direction. Just like a boss advocating safety standards, she says, a parent has to "act with integrity" and model the behavior she is trying to teach. It is also important to admit one's mistakes and failures and try to make up for them.

Another lesson is gratitude. "Gratitude got me through the darkest days of my life," Barb says. She recalls the time when she had left her position at the school board, she had no job, and her second marriage was breaking up. She had also suffered two miscarriages in that marriage. At that point, she began a "gratitude journal"—at the end of the day, she would write down everything she was grateful for. Sometimes the day was so bad that she was only grateful that it had ended, but she wrote that down. "I am not by nature an optimist," Barb says, but she found the practice "fuelled my optimism." It is a practice she continues to this day. "Life is a precious gift," she says, and it needs to be valued.

Barb's biggest mistake is "trusting too readily." She recalls helping one woman who later tried to have her removed from her position, and giving business to another woman who refused to send any business Barb's way. Barb was puzzled. "I didn't see it as competition." But that weakness has proved to be a strength too, because it taught her a valuable lesson. She says she learned "to help others because you want to and not expect anything in return. Then you won't be let down."

PASSION

Finding her passion didn't come easily for Barb. "I was late finding it," she says, "and some of it is luck"—such as the TB spill that aroused her interest in occupational health and safety. One way to find your passion is by trial and error, "finding out what you don't like, and that leads you to what you do like."

Barb's best piece of advice is: "Listen to your heart, follow your passion, find something you love—and then you will never work a day in your life"—because it will be so enjoyable, it won't seem like work.

Barb finds great satisfaction in "making a difference in people's lives. I make sure people go home in one piece and have a good quality of life—and I get paid to do it, which is a bonus."

But the work is not easy. "Changing people's attitudes and behavior," she says "is an art, not a science."

She concludes, "I am very lucky to be in health and safety. It is a growing field. It is a field that needs young people with fresh ideas—and older people who mentor them and who stay young by pushing the envelope."

Helping Others to Be All They Can Be

Angela Sladen

Co-Founder and Publisher of Womanition
NuSkin Distributor

Angela's passion in life is to help others to be all they were created to be. She believes that every person she comes in contact with is there for a reason; and that reason is so she can help them in whatever way she can. This passion is evident in both Angela's personal and professional life.

Growing up in numerous towns and cities in Canada has helped to shape Angela into whom she has become. Angela recalls being teased as a child and was ostracized by others because she was Aboriginal. But she says, "Life either makes or breaks you." For Angela, her childhood experiences made her even more determined to be who she wanted to be. It also helped to develop in her a compassion for others who might be struggling with feelings of inferiority because of class, gender, nationality, or education.

Angela also has a very supportive family. Her husband, Stan, of over twenty years, has patiently and supportively encouraged her to do just about anything she wanted. Growing up, her father, himself a victory story of residential school, encouraged all three of his daughters, telling them that they could do whatever they set their minds to do. Through his and her mother's encouragement, Angela took piano lessons to Grade Ten Royal Conservatory and participated in numerous sports. School was not her strong point but now that she is an adult, she is continually taking courses, learning new things and always trying to improve herself. Angela describes her mother as having a gentle, kind spirit—a good balance to the drive and determination of her father. She always has a kind and encouraging word to say. Angela's sisters are very dear to her and although they live in another city, they visit often.

Another person who continues to be an inspiration to Angela is her dad's foster mom who, after her husband died, took in numerous delinquent boys. This woman, who is ninety-five years young, has devoted her whole life to serving other people and has both blessed many others and has been blessed because of it. Angela also has many long-time friends who have stuck by her, some even offering to babysit her ten children so she and her husband could go on a much-needed vacation alone.

The most important thing to Angela is her faith. Growing up in a Christian family was the foundation for who she is today. Not that she didn't wander from her faith as a teenager but, as an adult who has returned to her faith, she believes that "your convictions determine who you are, what you do, and why you do it, and that we are here to serve, not to be served."

Another of Angela's life-changing experiences was supporting the family (four children) while her husband, Stan, went to university for four years to become an engineer. To support the family, Angela babysat two children during the day, home-schooled two of her children, taught piano in the early evening, and was a Tupperware and Silk Plant distributor in the later evening. The family had a tight budget but lots of love, fun, and ingenuity. For example, instead of taking a vacation every year, they bought a family pass to West Edmonton Mall for the summer and used it almost every weekend. They also bought a shell of a trailer and went camping several times a year.

The children never knew they did not have any money. Angela's parents were also very supportive financially during this time. "I remember that Christmastime was a challenge. We barely had enough money to live, let alone buy presents for our four children. Stan and I didn't buy gifts for each other until we were married six years. The wonderful thing was that living in St. Albert, a very prosperous city, we were a recipient of the county's Christmas gift packages. Our kids have never had so many presents as they did when we received those gifts. We had to give some away! The experiences of those four years taught me that we can do anything we set our minds to do, especially if we know failure is not an option. I also learned that I have a God who will take care of me no matter what."

Shortly after Stan finished University, they decided to become foster parents. For Angela, making the decision to become a foster mom was an easy one since her father had been a foster child and her mom and dad were also foster parents.

According to the medical world, all of Angela's foster children had varying degrees of fetal alcohol syndrome and several other "handicaps". So Angela chose to be a stay-at-home mom and homeschool her five children along with her five foster children. Her main concern was that the children would be teased or labeled and start to believe they were "different" from others, and use that as an excuse for poor behavior or academic laziness. The investment in her children's lives has paid off. Her oldest foster daughter is a very talented hair stylist with an elite salon. Her oldest foster son is attending university and was on the university swim team. All of the foster children still call Stan and Angela mom and dad and come home for special occasions. Angela still has two children at home, an eleven-year-old, and an eighteen-year-old who is attending university. Angela has also been blessed with a son-in-law and three grandchildren, ages five, four, and two, who live close by.

While still homeschooling, Angela took some nutrition courses and became a registered nutritional consultant. She ran a home-based business for several years offering nutritional counseling to many clients from Canada and the United States. After the family moved and her children were enrolled in a private school, Angela opened a women's full-service gym called Female Fitness. There she was able to use her training in nutrition and, after taking courses in personal training, was able to offer her clients both nutritional counseling and personal training.

Angela was ready to move on to a new challenge after four years. She had expanded the square footage within a year and had pretty much used up all the opportunities for expansion. Although she had enjoyed the challenge of building the business from scratch, once it was well established, she found herself losing interest.

It was while she was still the owner of Female Fitness that she met Dorothy Briggs. They first formed a professional relationship through personal training and it turned into a strong friendship which then turned into a business partnership. Together they developed Womanition Inc., an organization that supports those in need. A couple of the projects that Womanition supports is Opportunity International, an organization that provides microloans to people in developing countries enabling them to begin a business and find their way out of poverty, and a local women's shelter that works to change the lives of abused and/or addicted women.

The heart of Womanition is to support women and children in need. They do that through donations to local charities in every city the *Womantion* magazine is published.

The business of Womanition is to support and promote women in business. This is done through providing various marketing and networking opportunities. One such opportunity is to own a *Womanition* magazine franchise. Their goal is to have a *Womanition* magazine in every major city in every province and state.

You can also join the Womanition online community. Benefits include: lessons from the best and most successful leaders in all industries, exclusive discounts and promotions, a chance to market your products, opportunity to become published, and other networking occasions such as the upcoming Womanition-sponsored educational networking lunches.

Angela is also co-publisher of the Edmonton *Womanition* magazine. There are 20,000 copies of this magazine distributed in Edmonton each year with a readership of over 80,000. There is also a Southern Alberta magazine and one will soon be up and running in Fort McMurray. *Womanition* magazine runs features of professional and business women as well as articles that are relevant to all women.

In addition to her other responsibilities in Womanition Inc., Angela recently lived out the mission statement of helping to support and promote women in business by assisting the publisher of Southern Alberta *Womanition* magazine. Carmen LaFrance had been experiencing some health issues that left her unable to work for several months. Angela and Dorothy Briggs offered their support, which was gratefully acknowledged by Carmen in the magazine's Letter from the Publisher's Desk: "The true colors of Womanition came shining bright, and they went beyond the call of duty. They truly are amazing, fun, and a joy to do business with."

Right after Angela sold Female Fitness, she was approached by a good friend about another business, NuSkin Enterprises. This time though, it was helping people look ten to seventeen years younger, become healthier than they've ever been, and offering them a chance to make their fortune in part-time hours. She jumped right in with both feet and has had amazing success. Angela found NuSkin to be a great fit for her as it is an international company, and she loves to travel. As a professional distribution leader, Angela helps to develop teams who market anti-aging technologies and products that have immediate results to fifty-one countries and is part of a quickly growing global network of over 750,000 active independent distributors.

Using scientific advances from innovators in the fields of dermatology, ethnobotany, and nutritional and cosmetic sciences, they develop products that support the health and longevity of skin and hair. Their products are the only scientifically proven products to deal with the sources of aging, not just the signs or symptoms. The European Galvanic Spa is a very popular product in the NuSkin line. It has been named the "wrinkle iron" because it produces dramatic results in only minutes by showing a marked difference in the lines and wrinkles on a person's face. NuSkin also has the only product guaranteed to bring the elastin in a person's face back to that of a twenty-year-old. They also own the patented rights to AgeLoc, the only product that instantly reduces the enzymes responsible for aging. Most have a money-back guarantee, which was also an attractive feature to Angela.

Angela was also attracted to NuSkin because of their commitment to serving those around the world. They have established a non-profit organization called Force for Good Foundation. This Foundation has donated more than 15 million dollars to projects around the world. Their motto is to "create a better world for children by improving human life, continuing indigenous cultures, and protecting fragile environments." They also partner with the Epidermolysis Bulosa Medical Research Foundation (EBMRF). EB is a painful, genetically-inherited skin disorder that is often fatal to babies within the first few months after birth. EBMRF supports research for a cure and treatment for EB at Stanford University School of Medicine. Through NuSkin's other non-profit foundation, Nourish the Children, they have fed over 150 million children around the world.

What keeps this busy mother and grandmother motivated? "Helping people—that's what keeps me going,"

Although Angela says, "I will do everything I know to help people be successful," she cautions that she "won't do it for them. Investing time and effort is a necessary component of success. If people have a strong enough motivation, they will put in that effort."

"People can be successful at anything they do if they have a strong enough 'why'." Angela discovered this while she was owner and personal trainer at Female Fitness when she assisted her clients to find the motivation they needed to develop a healthy lifestyle. Angela believes that you need to discover the real reason people want to be successful before you can help them. When prospecting for new leaders, she will take them out individually for coffee and spend time getting to know them. Angela believes, "Building relationships is the key to a strong, successful, growing business." It is her goal to go for coffee with at least three new people each week.

Education is an important component of success but Angela maintains that "Knowledge is not power; application is power." It's not how much you know but what you do with that knowledge—how you apply it in achieving your life's goals. For young people who wish to prepare themselves for success, Angela advises that they aim to do what they want to do, regardless of how much money they will make doing it. "If you do something well, you will end up getting paid well to do it." Angela believes there are typically several things that a person feels passionate about. The more passions that can be combined in any endeavor or undertaking, the more successful that endeavor will be. People become frustrated, angry, and lose hope when their true passions are not being lived out in their lives.

Angela also believes in delegation, delegation, delegation. Delegating a weakness involves giving away those tasks that drain your energy so you have more time to devote to the things that increase your energy. For example, Angela confesses that she dislikes doing bookkeeping so she hires someone else to do it. This leaves her free to do what she does best—helping women become successful in business.

How does a person discover what her passions are? Angela suggests that you look back to your childhood and see what it was that you did when no one was telling you what to do! For Angela, she remembers appreciating beauty and color. With her first camera, she took many pictures of hoar frost and other beautiful things found in nature. Her friends and family are always interested to see what color she has painted her house. She also remembers being a budding entrepreneur at a very young age, collecting "fool's gold" and selling it door to door!

Today, working with people is Angela's greatest joy. "Helping women develop their own business so they can live their dreams is the most rewarding part of what I do." Everyone has a different reason to strive for success. For some, it's a need for extra money. For others, it is an enthusiasm for the product that is being sold or a desire to help others. For many, it is a combination of the above reasons. Angela feels it is her privilege to find out what "drives" people, what they dream about, what keeps them up at night, and help them do what they really want to do.

Angela agrees with Zig Ziglar: "You will get all you want in life if you help enough other people get what they want." True success is helping others get what they want.

"It's all about the people," Angela says. "People before anything. People are what make life worth living. People are what matter."

I'll Show You

Brenda Topley
Owner, Black Sheep Design Studio

All her life, people have been telling Brenda Topley that she couldn't do things. It never discouraged her—it just made her more determined to succeed. Her driving force became: "I'll show you."

Brenda says, "Even as a kid, I felt I was misunderstood by my family." As the oldest of four children, she was always breaking the way for everyone else. "I was pretty rebellious. If I wanted something, I was going to get it, and I always got it, one way or another. It was determination. People used to say you're so lucky. I never used to think of it as luck. I used to say no, I just wanted something, so I went and got it … That's where 'I'll show you' came from."

Brenda wanted to be a nurse, but was discouraged when others said, "You could never be a nurse. Why would you be a nurse?" So the other dream she had back then was to get married and have children.

The family had a fire and lost their house when she was twelve. This made her very resourceful to get new clothing and things. She babysat night after night to earn money. Brenda left school in grade ten and went to Regina to find a job. She worked for Woolco for a year and then took a hairdressing course.

Marriage followed in 1967. When her oldest son was two, he contracted osteomyelitis as a result of a smallpox vaccination and spent two years in hospital. This was a very trying time. After three children, one hospitalized, and some difficult times, the marriage ended.

Brenda then headed to Calgary to be near her family and start a new life. Failure was not on option. "Being on my own with three kids, it was up to me to support them. If I didn't push myself, my kids wouldn't have eaten and wouldn't have had clothes." She went on social assistance for a few months until she could get re-established. Her family helped with babysitting and moral support and her father co-signed for a 100 dollar loan so she could buy a car. She convinced the federal government's Manpower department to finance secretarial training so she could find a job that would financially support her family.

People kept telling her she didn't have enough education or couldn't do certain jobs in an office. The manager at the first place she worked told her, "You'll never make it because you haven't the training to know what is going on." But she kept proving them wrong. When someone went on holidays, she would offer to fill in and learned new skills. She moved from one job to another, getting better and better positions. She also sold Mary Kay products for eight years to supplement her income. "When things were really tough, I would go out and sell another mascara to make enough money to put groceries on the table."

VISUAL LEARNING

"I was never very good in school, but I became extremely visual," Brenda says. "I was always watching what was going on, and I learned by watching. My grandmother had a saying, 'If you didn't learn something new today, you didn't have a good day.' That is a philosophy I live by today. I was always taking courses, and I never quit learning."

The way to learn, Brenda says, is not just from school but also from life. In the world, you learn how to survive and make things work. Even when she is teaching, she adds, "My students teach me."

Something Brenda's mother said has stayed with her: "You can never dream bigger than you can achieve." From that, Brenda learned, "You can dream all these dreams, and you can make them come true. It depends on how much you want it, how hard you are going to try to get it." Dreaming and achieving those dreams has become a central focus of Brenda's life.

Brenda follows a universal spirituality, which is an extremely important part of her life. She says, "I believe there is so much more out there."

Long before she had heard of the book *The Secret*, Brenda was already practicing its central message: If you dream about it, you can have it. "That's what I was doing all those years. Because I wanted it, I kept going and getting it, because I figured I deserved it." It is part of her "I'll show you" attitude.

For instance, after going through a second bad marriage and a number of other relationships, Brenda wrote out a list of what she wanted in a man—someone who communicated well, who loved her for who she was, and who loved her children. Within six months, she had met Stew. When he walked into the office where she was working, Brenda immediately thought, "I'm going to marry that man." It took from June to October to get him to take her out. They were married in April of the next year and have been happily married for twenty-three years. "We have a good life. We don't fight. We did all our fighting in our first relationships," Brenda says. The key is that she and Stew respect each other.

In fact, two years after her divorce from her first husband, the two of them sat down, had a talk, and out of respect for each other, they determined not to put their children in the middle as so many other divorced couples do. "Family is very important," she says. They became very good friends and did the best they could to raise their children to respect others. Unfortunately, her first husband died in 1986, three months after she married her present husband.

Some years before they met, Stew had been talked into buying a yarn shop. A couple of years after the purchase, it was discovered that the shop was deeply in debt to twenty-two creditors. Brenda took over the shop to try to resolve the issues. The problem was that she "didn't have any idea about how to knit" and she often had to ask a friend down the hall to show her how to do things. Brenda would also read instructions to customers and watch them as they followed the instructions; after the customers left, Brenda would try to visually reverse what the customer had done and learn how to do it herself. Brenda saw the store through that immediate financial crisis and kept it going another five years.

Brenda says, "Sometimes you get tough because you learn what it takes to survive. But inside I'm still very soft and vulnerable."

DISCOVERING ART

Brenda's current husband, Stew, tells her she *can* do things. "He is a huge encouragement. He believes in me 100 percent." Stew told her she had talent and should take some art classes. At first she didn't believe she could do it, but decided to try because she was very visual and when she was younger. "Mom was always doing crafts with us."

Brenda took a course from the city of Calgary on how to make tiles and also signed up at the College of Art in first year ceramics in 1995. She then took second year ceramics and many summer courses at Red Deer college gaining a solid background in art design. Working with clay was very frustrating for her. The clay would crack while it was being fired. When glazed, it would break, or the colors would come out wrong. "With clay, I never had full control," Brenda says, "but I learned how to be patient (a lesson still being worked on). It taught me a lot about what works and what doesn't work and how to stick with it."

Later she took a course on how to make clay busts, and she taught the course to others. "That's when I found out how much I liked to teach."

Five years ago, while Brenda and Stew took a painting course, they saw a sculpture in a window made out of a different material. Brenda asked the store owner what it was made of and if she was going to hold a class on how to make them. After taking the course, she made ten pieces in the next three weeks.

The new product was called Paverpol, developed by a woman named Jossy de Roode in the Netherlands ten years ago (www.paverpol.com) and which is now sold in seventeen countries. Paverpol is easy to work with and hardens in one day, which Brenda says provides "instant gratification." Once it has cured for two weeks, it is extremely durable. It can be left outside through a Prairie winter without the material deteriorating or the colors fading.

Brenda is now a certified instructor/trainer for Paverpol, and she is the distributor for Alberta, Saskatchewan, and Manitoba, operating out of her home in Red Deer, Alberta. She and two other distributors oversee all of Paverpol's operations in Canada. Brenda has trained seven other instructors who work with her. The product is still very new in Canada, and the distributors would like to train many more instructors and artists across the country.

Brenda finds great joy in mentoring others and encouraging them. "I've always loved teaching. There is nothing more rewarding than hearing people say, 'I can't do that,' and then teaching them how to do it, step by step. They go home with big smiles on their faces." Brenda says that also encourages them to think of other things in life they can do.

One of the reasons she has good people working with her in her business, Brenda says, is that she respects each of them for who they are and where they are at. "We all have a right to be the way we are."

Success at Sixty

Brenda's current business, Black Sheep Design Studio (www.bstdesignstudio.com), also came out of a dream. When she had the yarn shop, she began having a recurring dream of a little white house with a veranda. There were three black sheep in each of the windows on each side of the front door. When she went inside, the room was empty. The next room was also empty. When she began working in clay, the dreams came back, shelves appeared, and there were people running around in the back room but she couldn't see what they were doing. When she began working with Paverpol, the shelves in the first room filled up with statues, and the back room filled up with teachers and classes.

Brenda's greatest success came when a piece of Paverpol art she made was accepted into a juried show at the CFM art gallery in New York, along with the work of five other Paverpol artists.

Another accomplishment is raising her three boys, who have "grown into confident and successful men."

At sixty, Brenda is achieving the success she wants and began seeking at sixteen. She doesn't define success in terms of money but in terms of how she feels about herself, her work, and the people around her. "People grow old because they don't keep their minds and bodies active." She describes a holiday she and Stew took to Curacao in November 2008 to celebrate her sixtieth birthday. "I can only sit on a beach for half a day if I'm lucky. I can't sit still. My mind is constantly in motion and then I get bored."

Some time back, the TV program *Take Five at Noon* came out to Brenda's studio to do a short profile on her. When she saw the video, Brenda said it reminded her of someone. Then she realized it reminded her of the person she wanted to be. She says, "I made it. I am who I want to be, and I am proud of how it turned out."

"I made a lot of mistakes," Brenda adds, "but I would never change the things that happened in my past because those are the things that made me who I am today. If I hadn't had all those trials and tribulations, I wouldn't be where I am, and I wouldn't appreciate what I have. I love who I am today. I have a great life."

Brenda says her biggest mistake was listening to other people and not believing she could do things.

Brenda's best advice is, "Believe in yourself. Surround yourself with the people who will help get you there. Go for it, and don't let anyone or anything stop you." She adds, "What you put out in life, you get back tenfold. I wish for everyone to follow their dreams."

FINANCIAL FINESSE

Donna Worthington, CFP, EPC
Investment Planning Counsel,
Certified Financial Planner

In 1992 I made a career decision that would change my life forever. Not only would I become a partner in a financial planning firm but would eventually earn my way to serve my new-found profession on the national executive of the Canadian Institute of Financial Planners.

My career as a registered nurse had been exceptional and exciting. My positions had varied from casual nurse to nursing supervisor and from pediatrics and orthopedics to emergency and ICU. I also had the pleasure of serving in northern outposts and hospitals.

In fact, I met my husband of thirty-two years (a member of the RCMP) in a northern Alberta native community. After our marriage we had only two moves and came back to Edmonton where I grew up.

It was here that I went back to University to complete my nursing degree. In a teaching and learning course I was required to write and implement an educational program. "Clean Hands Dirty Hands", a health promotion program for young school children, was born. With corporate sponsorship, we had a team of nurses traveling from Nova Scotia to Vancouver Island presenting the program to schools and other health care professionals. In 2002 I received the YWCA Woman of Distinction award in Health and Medicine. My entrepreneurial spirit had emerged. I had the talent, nerve, and ambition to change careers. In 1998 I graduated from Grant MacEwan College from the "Certified Financial Planning Program."

Over the years, I have become very aware of the financial struggles of families, but of women in particular.

Here are just a few of the statistics:

- 9 out of 10 women at some point in their lives will be solely responsible for their own finances
- The average age of widowhood is 56 years
- Few women will celebrate their 30th wedding anniversary because of divorce
- The average woman spends 15 years of her career out of the paid work force caring for children and aging parents[1]
- For every year a woman stays home caring for a child, she must work 5 extra years to recover lost income, pension coverage, and career promotion[2]
- Women live on average 5 years longer than men[3] and have higher health care costs[4]

There is hope, but before things can improve, education, learning, and action must take place. Would you think of going to a dentist, lawyer, doctor, or an accountant without the proper education, training, or credentials? Settle for nothing less than an advisor with the "Certified Financial Planner" designation.

---

[1] Women's Institute for a Secured Retirement
[2] National Centre for Women & Retirement Research
[3] Statistics Canada
[4] Bureau of Census

FINANCIAL FINESSE OR "WHAT WOMEN WANT"

Ladies, it's not really "What Women Want" but more about "What Women Need."

What every woman needs is to put her trust in the hands of a professional financial planner. He or she should hold the Certified Financial Planner (CFP) designation. This identifies individuals who are dedicated to the highest level of professionalism in providing financial advice. The CFP credential assures that the planner adheres to internationally recognized standards of competence and ethical practice as set in Canada by the not-for-profit Financial Planners Standards Council (FPSC).

Financial planning is a process that determines how you can best meet your life goals through the proper management of your financial affairs. The key to effective financial planning is the ability to take into account all relevant aspects of your financial situation and to identify and analyze the interrelationships among sometimes conflicting objectives. It is this unique integration of knowledge and skills across a broad range of topics that distinguishes professional financial planning from other related financial advice.[5]

It is important to have a financial planner whom you like and trust.

Financial planning is a two-way process—an exchange, a partnership. Your financial advisor brings knowledge and experience while you bring an open-minded view of your financial situation. Financial planners deal with one of the most personal aspects of your life—your financial security.

---

[5] Financial Planners Standards Council, "Can We Talk" brochure

GETTING STARTED

Establish the engagement. You and your planner agree on the scope of the financial planning engagement. How is the planner compensated? What time frames are put in place? Are there any conflicts of interest? How is your confidentiality maintained? This is called the Letter of Engagement.

THE FINANCIAL PLANNING PROCESS

Personal financial planning focuses on the individual. In order to best serve an individual's needs, the professional financial planning practitioner employs The Total Financial Planning Process comprising these six distinct steps:

Step 1: Clarify Your Present Situation

The financial planner clarifies your present situation by collecting and assessing all relevant financial data such as lists of assets and liabilities, tax returns, records of securities transactions, insurance policies, will, pension plans, etc.

Step 2: Identify Goals and Objectives

The financial planner helps you identify both financial and personal goals and objectives as well as clarify your financial and personal values and attitudes. These may include providing for children's education, supporting elderly parents, or relieving immediate financial pressures which would help maintain your current lifestyle and provide for retirement. These considerations are important in determining the best financial planning strategy for you.

Step 3: Identify Financial Problems

The financial planner identifies financial problems that create barriers to achieving financial independence. Problem areas can include too little or too much insurance coverage, or a high tax burden. Your cash flow may be inadequate, or the current investments may not be winning the battle with changing economic times. These possible problem areas must be identified before solutions can be found.

Step 4: Recommendations

The financial planner provides written recommendations and alternative solutions. The length of the recommendations will vary with the complexity of your situation, but they should always be structured to meet your needs without undue emphasis on purchasing certain investment products.

Step 5: Implement Strategies

A financial plan is only helpful if the recommendations are put into action. Implementing the right strategy will help you reach the desired goals and objectives. The financial planner should assist you in either actually executing the recommendations, or in coordinating their execution with other knowledgeable professionals.

Step 6: Monitor and Review

The financial planner provides periodic review and revision of your financial plan to assure that the goals are achieved. Your financial situation should be re-assessed.[6]

WEALTHY WOMEN: WHAT THEY KNOW AND PRACTICE WHAT WE CAN LEARN FROM THEM

Becoming "financially independent" can be very dull, tedious, and even boring. It will not happen overnight and may take five, ten or even twenty years, depending on where you are

---

[6] Ativa Interactive, Concept Toolkit, www.ativa.com

today. One thing is for certain, everyone with the right dose of determination can succeed. For each of us, being wealthy has a different meaning based on our lifestyle goals.

Let us look at some of the practices of the wealthy:

1) They cover their risks by having proper and sufficient insurance for their car, home, life, and their ability to work. We all hear about life insurance to cover our debt should we die. We need enough disability insurance to cover a loss of income. Should we develop cancer, heart attack, or stroke, wouldn't it be nice to collect a lump sum to help us through these illnesses? This type of insurance is called critical illness insurance and can be purchased with a return of premium.

2) The wealthy dislike being in debt and prefer to pay off their credit cards monthly. Debt is not terminal but needs to be addressed immediately. Debt consolidation can be very helpful; however, continually consolidating debt into your mortgage is a one way trip to nowhere. You may never own your own home! Don't be fooled into a false sense of security. Over the years, we have seen many couples whose mortgage is now five times the original price of their home. Should interest rates go up or they lose their job, they could lose their home because they cannot afford their payments.

3) Wealthy women who want to maintain their lifestyle control their spending. In fact, some are coupon clippers and like to buy when things are on sale. They buy quality versus quantity. They meet their needs and curb their wants.

4) The wealthy tend to live in nice neighborhoods, somewhat older but well kept. They are proud of the equity they have built in their homes.

5) Wealthy women show pride in their cars, which they tend to keep a little longer than normal. The cars are well maintained, and are clean inside and out.

6) The wealthy use the professionals. They have a lawyer do their will, enduring power of attorney, and personal directives. No will kit for them—they want to be sure things are done right! They use an accountant and follow their advice. They have a financial plan done by a professional and keep to their plan, always revisiting it annually to be sure they are on track.

7) Wealthy women are philanthropic and give back to their community in time, talent, and treasure. Women tend to give smaller amounts to charities than men, but they give to more charities.

This is just a glimpse into some of the habits of the wealthy and those who want to get there sooner than later.

AFFLUENT BABY BOOMERS—ARE YOU PREPARED?

As the baby boomers grow closer to retirement, many are finding that they are ill prepared for the lifestyle sacrifices that they will need to make. They have a home that is paid for, two cars, many toys, and a lifestyle that they have become increasingly comfortable with. They enjoy the arts, travel, dining out—and they want it all to continue.

When faced with reality, at their desired retirement age, they will be short of cash.

So what went wrong? We are finding a wide range of problem areas and solutions.

The first problem area is that they underestimated their savings amount. They simply may not have saved enough to supplement their pension income. Often we are finding they have forgotten about inflation and taxes. Inflation has been relatively low over the past few years, averaging a little over 3 percent per year, but this can still diminish your purchasing power. Also, there are inevitable taxes. In retirement you are taxed on all your income sources which include pension income, Canada pension income, investment income, retirement savings income, and any earned income.

So what are the solutions?

1) They can choose to work longer. One to five years more of working means one to five years less of drawing on retirement savings. Working longer can also increase your CPP and private pension.

2) They can make a lifestyle choice for retirement that costs less. Not a very comforting thought. Giving up travel and the cottage at the lake may not be what they had envisioned retirement to be.

3) Many retirees are returning to the workforce, some to supplement their pension incomes and some to reinvent themselves. Retirement is becoming more about transition and new opportunities versus sitting on the porch in a rocker thinking of the past.

Whatever their choices, a new reality has hit, and it's not pleasant. As this first wave of baby boomers struggle and adjust, the next wave needs to wake up, take notice, and take action.

The way to financial independence and security starts with a comprehensive financial plan. To start, collect all your financial data which includes: monthly income and expenses, record of all debt and assets, last couple years of tax returns, all pension statements including CPP and private pensions, insurance policies, all investments and RRSP statements. If you have made a will, power of attorney and personal directive, make copies of these for your advisor.

Now what is it that you want for the future? Consider the number of years you plan to work and how long you think you will live (95 to 100 years is becoming more the reality). What do you think you will need for income in retirement? Can you live on 80 percent of what you have now? Do you have any specific plans for your retirement years?

Once you have your paperwork and thoughts together, seek the help of a professional financial planner. Choose one with the CFP (Certified Financial Planner designation). For a list of professionals in your area go to the FPSC.

Whether your financial planner is paid by commission, fee for service, or is an employee, it should make no difference in regards to his/her ability to do a financial plan for you. Any advisor with the CFP designation has the basic education, plus the required ongoing education, and errors and omissions insurance to serve the client in an ethical and professional manner.

Once you have chosen a planner ask what is required from you. Financial plans can take ten or more hours of work depending on how complicated your life is. For those clients who own businesses the plan can take considerably longer. This discussion should be formally addressed in a Letter of Engagement. It will address the time frames, what is required from you the client, disclose any conflicts of interest the advisor may have, the privacy policy, and how the advisor is compensated. The Letter of Engagement will also discuss the plans limitations and when reviews are to be conducted.

The advisor will provide you with a draft plan once he has received all the documents. Review it carefully. Have your goals been addressed? The recommendations then need to be discussed and the plan implemented. Reviews need to be annual or whenever there is a change in your life that requires adjustments.

1) In order for your financial plan to work, it needs to be implemented. Be diligent, follow through, and do not give in to temptation. Ignore hot market tips and remember that following the herd is not for you. If you have questions, call your financial advisor and not a friend. The road to financial security starts with having a well constructed financial plan.

2) Learn to manage your cash flows. Decipher your needs from your wants. Remember cash at the end of the month is better than month at the end of the cash. If you keep coming up short on cash you have only two choices: make more money or curb your expenses.

3) Pay off your credit card debt. Do you know the real cost of credit card debt? The 18 percent interest rate is being paid with after-tax dollars so you need to earn considerably more.

4) Buy RRSP's for both the initial tax deduction and the long-term savings benefit as they grow tax free. The basic idea is that your income will be less in retirement and you will be taxed at a lower rate. Once you have maximized your RRSP contributions each year, use your tax return to pay down your mortgage.

5) Cover your risks. Many of your risks will become evident when you do your financial plan. If you drive a car, you require car insurance. Many people neglect the need for disability, critical illness, long term care, and basic life insurance.

6) Use managed money portfolios for your investment needs. These portfolios are built to meet your needs based on:

your experience, risk tolerance, the length of time you have to invest, and the investment return you require. They are properly balanced to protect your savings in down markets as well as growth periods. Many companies offer products that have principle guarantees and market value guarantees.

7) Have you done proper will and estate planning? How old is your will, enduring power of attorney, and personal directive?

Now that you have your retirement plan in order you can relax but remember to revisit it on an annual basis or whenever there is a life-changing event.

People don't plan to fail at anything
but they frequently fail to plan.

Donna is a professional who holds the CFP and EPC (Elder Planning Counselor) designations. She is a member of the Canadian Institute of Financial Planners and sits on the national board of directors as second vice president. Donna does a limited number of speaking engagements each year.

For more information about Financial Finesse seminars, Business Building seminars, or personal financial planning, call Donna Worthington at (780)702-1551.

PHOTO INDEX

Jennifer Belland
4614 Macleod Trail South
Calgary AB T2G 5E8
Tel: 1-888-717-2517
www.albertamortgagequotes
.com/jenniferbelland

Page 21

Dorothy Briggs
Tel: 780-761-3000
www.womanition.com
www.servalldatasystems.com

Page 29

Photographer

Daphne Carlyle, MPA SPA
97 - 53250 Range Road 215
Ardrossan AB T8E 2B3
Tel: 780-922-4014
www.allaboutangels.net

Page 37

Jessie Arlone Davies
5111 - 17 Avenue NW
Edmonton AB T6L 1X6
Tel: 780-479-5787
Fax: 780-479-5787

Page 45

Kim A. Deep, CMA
7208 - 156 Avenue NW
Edmonton AB T5Z 2Z8
Tel: 780-483-4010
www.kidzmakecents.com

Page 53

Faith Grant
113 Haddow Close
Edmonton AB T6R 3W3
Tel: 780-431-9623
www.rejuvenationhealth.ca

Page 63

Deborah Kurach
152 - 11 Athabascan Avenue
Sherwood Park AB T8A 6H2
Tel: 780-416-2700
www.vervesalon.ca

Page 71

Carmen LaFrance
#63, 4307 - 130 Ave SE,
Suite 162
Calgary AB T2Z 3V8
Tel: 403-241-9209
www.womanition.com or
www.womanition.com/
connections/
calgary-connection/

Page 77

Barbara Lynn Semeniuk
2051 Tanner Wynd
Edmonton AB T5R 2R4
Tel: 780-431-1284
www.purcellenterprises.ca

Page 85

Angela Sladen
Ardrossan AB
Tel: 780-914-8079
www.womanition.com
www.angelasladen.nse-
dreams.com
angela.sladen@gmail.com

Page 93

Brenda Topley PPT
4 Burbank Close
Blackfalds AB T0M 0J0
Tel: 403-885-0476
www.bstdesignstudio.com

Page 101

Donna Worthington
CFP, EPC
905 - 10025 - 106 St.
Edmonton AB T5J 1G4
Tel: 780-702-1551

Page 109

Franchise Opportunities Available in Your City across Canada and the United States

Marketing to women is one of the single largest, untapped target markets in the world.

Owning your very own Franchise offers you:

- Opportunity to give to charitable organizations from generated revenue (in lieu of ongoing franchise fees)
- Relationships and growth opportunities with amazing businesswomen who have "been there-done that"
- Connections with other Franchisees to promote and encourage the development of your business.
- Recognition as a credible Business Owner.
- An opportunity to own a debt-free company within your first year of business.
- And much more!

Secure your territory now!
Call Franchise Owners Angela Sladen at 780-914-8079 or Dorothy Briggs at 780-761-3000

JOIN OUR ONLINE WOMANITION™ COMMUNITY

This is what you receive:

- Lessons from the best and most successful leaders in all industries
- Exclusive discounts, promotions and specials for member's only
- A chance to market your products / services to the other members
- Opportunity to "publish" yourself to gain credibility, recognition and become the "go-to" person in your industry
- Occasions to network and connect with other like minded individuals
- And much, much more!

Go to www.womanition.com
and click on Join Our Team

*How would you like to be your
own boss and part of a growing
dynamic team of
businesswomen?*

*Be a publisher of the most "influential"
local women's magazine on the market!*

WOMANITION™

Dedicated to Supporting and Promoting Women
in Process

By Women ... For Women ... Supporting Women

The *Heart* of Womanition™ is to Support
Women and Children in Need.

The *Business* of Womanition™ is to Support and
Promote Women in Business.